JOURNEY OF GRACE PUBLISHING

HOME

Finding Hope in Your Journey

Always be prepared to give an answer to everyone
who asks you to give the reason for the hope that you have.
1 Peter 3:15 (NIV)

Ernest K. Gober, Author
Julie Gober, Co-Author & Compiler

Journey of Grace Publishing

CONROE, TEXAS

Editing and cover design by Harvest Creek Design.
Cover photograph by Photography by Joyelle (www.photographybyjoyelle.com)
Illustrations by Josh Gober, Shelby Gober, Jacob Gober, Aiden Gober, Peyton Dauzat, and Hannah Dauzat, son and grandchildren of Ernest Gober. Used by permission.

All scripture quotations, unless otherwise indicated, are taken from the *New King James Version*. Copyright© 1979, 1980, 1982 by Thomas Nelson, Inc. Used by permission. All rights reserved.

Scripture quotations marked (NIV) are taken from The Holy Bible, *New International Version*® NIV®. Copyright© 1973, 1978, 1984, 2011 by Biblica, Inc.™ Used by permission of Zondervan. All rights reserved worldwide. www.zondervan.com The "NIV" and "New International Version" are trademarks registered in the United States Patent and Trademark Office by Biblica, Inc.™

Journey of Grace Publishing
3915 West Davis, Suite 130
PMB 134
Conroe, TX 77304

Home/Ernest Gober. —1st ed.
ISBN-13: 978-1-7333498-0-2

Printed in the United States of America

DEDICATION

This book is dedicated to the Lord Jesus Christ, who rescued me and to my precious family who encouraged me to journal the stories they've heard about how He changed my life. It's written with special thanks to Charles and Shirley, my wife's parents, and their children for accepting me into their family with unconditional love. To my sister, who was always there for me. To Mike, Mary, Jeff, and Kim for opening their hearts and home like they did. To the White family who loved me into the kingdom and helped guide me home to Jesus.

It's written with sincere appreciation to all those who reached out to extend a hand up along the way. Some of you had a positive word or act of kindness in looking out for me as I grew up. Some of you had words of wisdom or encouragement to share as I grew in faith. Some of you prayed for me, and I didn't even know it. My life was never the same because of your touch.

This is my story, as I remember it. There will be things that make you laugh, things that make you cry, and things that may even make you mad. There will be things that make some of you shake your head and say, "Only you, Ernie." If you're struggling with life today, I pray it blesses your heart and strengthens your spirit. Hopefully, after reading it, you'll be glad you did.

—ERNIE GOBER

ACKNOWLEDGMENTS

WRITING A BOOK is a bigger adventure than I ever imagined. It requires more hours than you'll probably ever believe and more knowledge than just one person could ever know. If not for the help of some very special people, this book may have never been printed so this page is for them.

To our children, Joy and Josh—for all of your help from illustrations, edits, graphics, and beyond, thank you. You are our world, and you are always there for us. Having your love, support and encouragement means everything. We are so truly blessed, and you are truly loved.

To Brent and Marie—two of the most precious children we could have ever inherited by marriage. Thank you for the many hours you allowed us to work on this book together, your ideas and your words of encouragement. You have such a special place in our hearts.

To our grandchildren—Shelby (age 15), Jake (age 13), Aiden (age 12), Peyton (age 7), and Hannah (age 5). Thank you for all of those sweet butterfly drawings. Each one is uniquely you, and a treasure to us, just like you are. May the changes in your lives take you to beautiful places.

To my mom, Shirley—you have always been our biggest fan and greatest supporter. Somewhere along the way, you also became our most trusted friend and advisor. Thank you for being who you are and for all you do.

To our friend, mentor and the pastor who married us, Dave Reddoch—Thank you for the helpful info that got this project started, the encouraging words along the way, and...thanks for tying that knot really tight when you married us!

To our editor, Teresa Granberry—Thank you for your professional advice, edits and encouragement. We truly believe God led us to you.

Ernest K. Gober
1956-2018

*But none of these things move me; nor do I count my life
dear to myself, so that I may finish my race with joy,
and the ministry which I received from the Lord Jesus,
to testify to the gospel of the grace of God.*
Acts 20:24

FOREWORD

ANYONE WHO KNEW ERNIE GOBER knew of his
testimony. He told his stories over and over again to
anyone who would lend an ear. Most of us indulged
his repetition because we loved his stories as much as
we loved him. We teased that he would tell his stories
to a doorpost if it would listen, and there may have
been a small measure of truth to that possibility.

Ernie's stories are a testimony to the loving nature
of a God who gave Himself to save us from the
consequences of our sins. They tell about the power
of prayer and the ability of God to keep us safely
within His care even though we wander and may not
know He's with us. They testify of the strength found
in brotherly love and the good that happens as faith
becomes an action word. They demonstrate the hope
that springs from a second chance and the
transformation that occurs within a life reformed.

Those who listened knew these stories were more
than just words to Ernie. His testimony was both his
life and lifestyle. We were entertained by his sense
of humor and inspired by his passion. He challenged
us all to live a life worthy of our calling, look for
deeper ways to trust God and follow in the footsteps
of Jesus with every step of our daily walk. That is how
he lived.

He was diagnosed with pancreatic cancer on
October 12, 2018. On the day his doctor told him that
he may have only six months to live, Ernie took his
family out for dinner. The waitress asked if we were
celebrating an occasion. We all looked at each other

speechless, but Ernie quickly responded, *"Yes, we're celebrating life!"*

It wasn't that Ernie never allowed life to pull him down. He had feelings and emotions just like we do. It was that Ernie refused to stay down. He knew God was able to do big things, so he chose to focus on what God could do. He knew where God had brought him from and was determined to think of what God might bring him to.

In the end, he knew God would bring him to Himself, so he purposed not to fear death. He often said, *"This world is not our home; we're only passing thru."* Before he journeyed from this life, he told us, *"Death is inevitable. It comes to us all, but it is not an end. It's just a change. So, when you see a butterfly, think of me."*

A life forever changed thru Jesus Christ. A home forever with Him in a place that knows no sin or sorrow. These are the reasons for the hope that gave Ernie such passion for living.

Ernie started drafting his testimony into book form several months before learning of the cancer. He was unable to complete it before his death on November 11, 2018, just one month after diagnosis. His family feels privileged to be able to finish this goal for him. The stories are not consecutive and will take you randomly through some of the memories of his life as he remembered them.

Home was not always a steady or safe place for Ernie. Memories from his childhood often brought faces and places that left him feeling unloved, unwanted, or unworthy. On the contrary, he came to learn he was loved with a love that defies all understanding. His story is a message of hope, and his desire was to leave you encouraged by his words. Our goal was to compile his message in a way that he would have liked for you to hear it.

Each time he began to tell one of his stories to us again, we jokingly told him we had his stories numbered. Today, they truly are.

Sleep in peace with Jesus, Ernie.
You are forever my always.
With all my love,
Julie

ERNIE'S STORIES

STORY NUMBER 1

THE BEER HOUSE BAR

*"To everything there is a season, a time for
every purpose under Heaven."*
ECCLESIASTES 3:1

WHEN I WAS A KID, maybe eight or ten years old, my parents ran a bar called the Beer House. There were often motorcycle riders from two or three biker clubs hanging out there at a time. They would get drunk and fight with each other and some of their fights were pretty bad. We watched them fight in the parking lot almost every night. People got stabbed, shot, beat up and everything else there. After closing, they would move the bikes out back and party all night long.

The bar served food from the kitchen like roast beef sandwiches and bar-b-que. A favorite menu item was Mom's fried chicken. She fried it up and put it inside the oven to keep it warm. That oven was full, from top to bottom and side to side. Sometimes the kids helped serve the food and wash beer glasses. When the police came, which was fairly often, we ran to our room in the back and locked the door. The bar had what was called go-go dancers. The ladies couldn't dance naked like some bars do today, so they wore bikinis. Sometimes my brother and I would be in the back room watching TV, and they would come change in the room while we were there. They didn't pay any attention to us, and we didn't pay any attention to them. Well, unless they were really cute.

One night, everyone was super drunk, and a lady was there with her husband. She went on stage and started dancing with the girls. She started removing her clothes, so my dad had to get her off the stage. When he tried, her husband went up there and slugged my dad. Big mistake! Some bikers grabbed the guy and took him outside. Dad got the lady off the stage, but then she was mad because her husband didn't stop him.

She was too drunk to realize what was really going on. The bikers had chained her husband to the back of a three-wheel bike and drug him to an alley down the street. In the meantime, his wife went out to their car and got a tire tool out of the trunk. She started busting out their car's lights and windows. She flat tore it up. While she was doing that, the bikers came back dragging her husband behind their bike. He was all banged up and didn't look like he was breathing. She freaked out and started screaming and swinging at the bikers.

About that time, someone came running out of the bar saying, *"Let's get out of here! The police are coming!"* They all got on their bikes and drove away while her husband laid in the parking lot with her crying over him. We didn't hear if the guy lived or died, but things like this happened all the time there. I saw more stuff in that bar than any kid should have ever seen, but our life there seemed normal. I didn't know other kids didn't live this way.

On another night, my brother was asleep in our room. Our room was the only one with a ceiling built over the room so no one could get in there if it was locked. My parents told us to keep the door locked but I got hungry and went to the kitchen for a snack. I forgot to lock the door and this drunk biker walked into our room. He thought my brother was a girl lying there all covered up and climbed in bed with him. He grabbed my brother on the bottom and my brother came alive. My brother grabbed a ball bat next to the bed and started hitting the guy. We heard screaming and ran to see what was going on. When my brother saw me, he started after me with the bat, but Dad stopped him.

Home didn't really seem like it should be any different than what it was when I was growing up.

My brother and I would clean the bar after it closed. We vacuumed, mopped, wiped tables and picked up beer glasses from the floor and off the pool tables. Sometimes there was money lying around, so it didn't seem so bad to clean. Some nights we didn't find anything but knowing we might made cleaning up feel a little better even though we hated it. Sometimes I stole beer to sell to my friends from the back door. Other times we just drank together instead, even as kids.

The bar was a crazy place and a crazy life, but we survived it. Home didn't really seem like it should be any different than what it was growing up. When you think of home you might recall happy memories, but the word rarely brought good thoughts for me. It took a while to figure out what home should be like. I've lived many places, including where there was no *home* to be found at all. This book is just a little of my story.

STORY NUMBER 2

THIS IS ME

"And we know that all things work
together for good to those who love God, to
those who are the called according to
His purpose."
ROMANS 8:28

PROBABLY BEFORE you hear about things like our home in the bar, you should know a little about where my life began. So, hi. My name is Ernie, and this is the story of my life. At least part of it, as best I can remember it. Some things have been forgotten. It's possible some memories have been blocked by choice. They weren't all good so it's probably best some things are not thought about at all anyway. And it's possible some memories may be confused, especially since we did a lot of drugs when I was younger.

The little town of Cushing, Oklahoma, was so small it almost wasn't there when I was born in 1956. It's still small today, in spite of its role in the oil industry with all of its connecting pipelines. I was pretty small on arrival there, too, weighing only three pounds, nine ounces and twenty-eight days premature. Those first twenty-eight days in the hospital helped prove how old I really was later on. Growing up, Mom always said I was born in 1955 and the birth year 1956 on my birth certificate was wrong. But the hospital bill and payment records we found after my mom died showed the birth year was indeed 1956. I got to turn twenty-one twice. My mom's memory must have been a little confused, too. Still, wouldn't you think most mothers would remember the day their child was born, especially one who spent their first month in a hospital crib away from mom? Oh, well.

Grandpa didn't want to come see me in the hospital. He said a baby that small couldn't live. He was wrong though, and he carried me around in the palm of his hand after they brought me home. Life was a fight right from the start, so I learned how to survive early. We all have challenges to overcome in life. Yours are probably different than mine, but you know what they are.

Sometimes the obstacles in our life don't seem fair. We may not have done anything to cause them, and we may not deserve what happened to us. Being born small was just the first of many challenges I would have to overcome in this life, but there was a way to win. Hopefully, you will find strength for whatever battles you may be facing in the pages of this story.

Life wasn't always challenging. Our family lived in a nice home in Oklahoma City when I was very young. Family included my parents, a sister and two brothers. Actually, my mom had two children from a previous marriage so there was my older half-sister and half-brother. Then they had my brother and I was the youngest.

Our house had a long driveway and a garage. There was a big tree beside the driveway. One day Dad decided to cut it down, so a few men came over to help him chop that big old tree. They attached ropes to guide it so it wouldn't fall on the house.

Then they had the problem of how to get that huge stump out of the ground. My father worked on it for a while. He must have lost that battle because the stump was there beside our driveway as long as we lived in that house. That's how some battles are. We may not win them all, but we can certainly try our best.

There were plenty of rough, unhappy, bad times in my life, and we could probably talk for days and days about them. There are many reasons to blame most of those bad things on the other people in my life, too. Actually, I can only remember a few things from my childhood and most of them are not so good.

My parents started drinking heavily when I was about six years old, and our lives took a turn for the worse because of it. They started coming home drunk every night. They would spend all their money drinking and then wake up the next day arguing over the money they blew the night before.

One day, my mom and dad were fighting on the way home from the grocery store when she started throwing grocery sacks out of the car window because she was mad at my dad. How crazy is that? When we got sick, they would send some drunk to the house to take care of us. It was really more like we took care of him, so we learned to take care of ourselves instead. Soon my parents started managing the clubs they drank in and life got even tougher.

It would be easy to blame others for the bad things in my life, but the truth is that I wasn't such a good kid either. I know my parents had a lot of trouble to deal with while raising me. They kicked me out of the house at about thirteen years old, and I was happy to get out.

Did I ever want to go back home? Sure, but it wouldn't work. Life at that time was confusing and painful. Home wasn't a word with a clear meaning, but it wasn't all my parent's fault. They had a bad drinking problem, and their priorities weren't right. That is true. But the bad attitude and the drugs they were dealing with on my end didn't help. My parents and I both had a lot to learn.

God was there even when I didn't know Him and didn't deserve Him. We all have bad things to deal with in life. Some of our *bad* is some really bad stuff and sometimes we have a lot of *why* questions. That's okay. Sometimes answers are not easy. Sometimes there will be no answers in this lifetime.

But God is still a good God. He is there working on our behalf even when we cannot see Him. He wants good things for us even when home is not what we think it should be.

This is my testimony of how God loved me and changed me. I'm living proof of what He can do. He's able to use all the bad things we go through in life to reach us and He can use them to accomplish good things for us when we let Him. He was there for me. He is there for you.

ABOVE: A note Ernie's mom wrote in his baby
book stating his birth year as 1955.
The correct date of birth is May 25, 1956.

ABOVE: A Cub Scout application completed by
Ernie's mom during third grade (about 1964) with
the wrong birth month. She entered his
date of birth as June 25, 1956.

BIRTHDAY NUMBER FIVE

"No discipline seems pleasant at the time,
but painful. Later on, however, it produces
a harvest of righteousness and peace for
those who have been trained by it."
HEBREWS 12:11 NIV

LIKE I SAID, life was pretty normal when I was young. My parents threw a party for my fifth birthday. Today, birthday parties are a big deal with reservations for a crowd every year at a fun place with really cool things like bounce houses or laser tag.

Back in the day, birthday parties didn't come very often, and they were nothing fancy. They were usually at your house with a few friends, birthday cake and some ice cream. Since you didn't get to have a party every birthday, kids got pretty excited when they got to have some party cake. It usually meant there would be presents to open!

This year, Mom said we were going to have a party for my birthday. She baked cupcakes and went to the store for ice cream. She was planning for a few friends and family, but I had something bigger in mind. The entire neighborhood got a visit from me and every kid got a personal invitation to the party.

Guess what happened? Yes, they all showed up. There were quite a few extra kids at our house that day

27

expecting birthday cake. Mom was surprised, and she was also very mad. At me!! Can you imagine?

Dad went to the store to get more cake and ice cream while all the kids enjoyed the party. All the kids except for me. A spanking was what they gave me for my birthday that year. Then they told me to return all the presents. No presents?

Presents was the whole reason those kids were invited. I told them they couldn't come unless they brought one so that was a sad birthday. It made me mad to return those gifts, but that birthday lesson has never been forgotten. It didn't seem fair at the time, but I understood later.

Selfishness and ungratefulness are not good attitudes. My parents wanted me to learn to be considerate and appreciative. These were traits my own children would need to understand later, too. How can we teach others about things we've never learned ourselves?

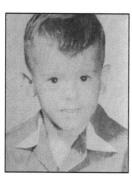

Ernie at about 5 years old

It was a hard lesson learned that day, but it was just the first of many lessons to learn as I grew up. As hard as this is for us to understand or accept, sometimes God knows we need to learn hard lessons as adults, too. Our human nature is selfish and ungrateful at times. Sometimes we're even worse and it causes us trouble.

If you're in a hard spot today, look for Him. Ask Him to guide you. He wants to provide peace for your troubled soul.

MY REDHEADED KINDERGARTEN GIRLFRIEND

*"When I was a child, I spoke as a child,
I understood as a child, I thought as a
child; But when I became a man, I put
away childish things."*
I CORINTHIANS 13:11

IN KINDERGARTEN, I had a little girlfriend or at least we thought we were girlfriend and boyfriend because we kissed a lot. She was cute, and she had the shiniest red hair ever seen. She lived right across the street from our house, so we spent a lot of time together in school and playing around the neighborhood.

We also got into trouble together. There was a big tree nearby with branches that hung over the road. We would climb up there with the mud pies we made and drop them on cars as they drove by. We sat where we thought the cars couldn't see us, but one day we got caught and had to wash a man's car.

Life was good for a while as a little boy. Mom and Dad owned a little house on a nice street. There was a man down the road who knew everyone on the block. We called him Doc but don't really know why. We didn't know his real name. He asked all the parents when their kids' birthdays were.

You know, sometimes it's the smallest things that make the biggest difference.

On each kid's birthday, he would fill his old pickup with hay and take us all for a hayride around the neighborhood. It was fun and we thought he was COOL! You know, sometimes it's the smallest things that make the biggest difference.

One time my parents took us out to look at little baby chicks for Easter. Back then, stores dyed the baby chickens different colors at Easter: pink, yellow, blue, red, and purple. We were able to pick whichever one we wanted and take it home.

The sad part is that when the little chicks grew up, they became dinner. We watched out the window in shock as my mom placed a broomstick on their little necks and pulled their feet until the heads popped off. Blood was everywhere. We just sat there and cried. It broke my heart, and I didn't want a baby chicken for Easter anymore.

Back to my red-headed girlfriend. We were curious kids. We had watched adults kissing and decided if it was okay for them, it was okay for us. So, we would hide in her garage to kiss. I'm sure you've heard the rhyme about two kids sitting in a tree.

You know: K-I-S-S-I-N-G, first comes love, then comes marriage, then here she comes with a baby carriage.

Well, we only got as far as K-I-S-S-I-N-G. We were way too young to think about anything else, but we kissed a lot.

The strange thing is that she always brought a box of tissues. Every time we kissed, she blew snot from her nose. It was pretty gross, but I thought it was normal since she was my first kiss.

Can you imagine how it felt when I found out it wasn't? When I asked the next girl why she didn't blow snot out of her nose, she laughed at me. How embarrassing! You're probably laughing now too but it was a big relief to a young boy to know kissing didn't have to be like that.

As a young man, it was a relief to learn a lot of the unpleasant things that seemed like a normal part of life didn't have to be that way. Thank God there were better things planned for me. There are good things ahead for you, too. Sometimes all it takes to see His plan is a little patience.

LITTLE GRAY SUBMARINE

"And this commandment we have from
Him: that he who loves God must love
his brother also."
I JOHN 4:21

HOW MANY OF YOU remember things that happened with your brother or sister when you were little? I remember this one time that my brother made me really mad. Has your sibling ever made you *really* mad? So mad you just had to get them back? I mean, to the core mad. Well, my brother did that a lot and I felt like I had to get him back a lot, too, especially this time.

I don't remember who got it for us. Maybe my mom got it or maybe it came from someone else. It came in the mail, and it was really cool. It was a submarine. Yes, a submarine! It was just a small toy made of cardboard, kite sticks and paper. It was gray with black lettering and had windows and doors drawn on it. The bottom was open so it could fit over your head.

It also had a hatch on the top that opened up, just like a real submarine would. We played with it while imagining we were riding underwater in a real submarine. We had so much fun with it.

We were supposed to share it, but my brother, like most big brothers, decided to hog the toy submarine. That made me really, really mad. Now, I was a kid then and a lot older now. My memory could be a little fuzzy so it might be possible that I was just really impatient and maybe that made it seem like my brother was being really selfish with the time we were supposed to be sharing with the toy submarine. It seemed real to me at the time though, so my temper was pretty hot.

Even as a kid, I was a bit crazy and definitely crazy jealous of that little gray submarine that day. While he was sitting inside of it with the top closed, I decided to douse the thing with gasoline and light it with a match. Now, remember it was only made of cardboard, paper and kite sticks so it went up in flames in just a matter of seconds. It disappeared in a flash with nothing left but ashes.

My brother was okay, but now he was mad. He jumped up from the pile of ashes that used to be a submarine and ran after me. He chased me but didn't catch me. My little legs were too fast for him. Thank goodness! He might have hurt me.

Loving my brother has become more important to me since that day. I didn't understand it then and honestly, not for a long time after, but I understand it more now. My brothers and sister had their own share of hurt growing up, but together we were a team.

Others have heard this story since that day, including my own children, and it makes some people laugh to hear what a crazy kid I was. It's a funny story, but my brother wasn't laughing with me that day. I've done other things that hurt him, and that thought isn't a pleasant one now. I'd like to say, *"I'm sorry for all the things I put you through, brother, and thanks for being there for me. I love you more than you might know."*

You may fight with your brother, too. Sometimes he won't seem very loveable and he'll probably think the same about you. You won't always understand each other, and you won't always agree. But he's your family and he's a more important part of your life than you might realize today. So, I encourage all of you to love your brothers and sisters, too.

You might be thinking I wouldn't say this if I knew *your* brother. Now, let me say, my half-brother didn't give me or anyone else in his life any good reason to love him. He did some really awful, unspeakable things to many people, including some children. There were only a handful of people present at his funeral, and I was one of them.

Loving my brother has become more important to me since that day.

Yes, I know your brother. You may not like him, and he may not be a likable person. But I know you need to forgive him, and you need to love him in spite of who he is. He needs Jesus, and what your brother is giving you is a lesson on how to love like Jesus loves us. We did nothing to deserve His love or forgiveness, but He freely gives it anyway.

Holding on to the anger and resentment you're feeling toward your brother will turn you into the kind of person you dislike one day. So, pray for your brother and forgive your brother. Pray for yourself to be able to love others like Jesus does. You'll be amazed at what doing this will do within you.

OUR NEIGHBORHOOD PARK

"So, teach us to number our days, that we
may gain a heart of wisdom."
PSALM 90:12

LIKE MOST KIDS, we had a favorite park that we all hung out at during the summer. We played checkers, hopscotch, chess, and other games. The park had a pool so we could swim and lay around getting a suntan. We were friends so we liked to do something special for each other sometimes while we were hanging out.

There was a watermelon patch down the street from the park. We didn't have money to buy a melon, so I snuck over to steal one. Then I snuck into the park before it opened and put the melon in the pool so it would be cold when everyone got there.

There were some things I had hidden in the bushes for cooking: a skillet, a two-burner propane camping stove, some tongs and cornmeal. With a gunny sack and gig, I headed to the pond at the fairground to catch some bullfrogs. Then I threw them in the gunny sack to take back to the park to fry with a cornmeal batter for us to eat.

Frying frog legs is easy. After gigging, you cut off the back legs, skin them and pull out the nerve. If you don't pull out the nerve, they'll jump around in the pan while they're frying. We took the watermelon from the pool and cut it to go along with the frog legs. We had a feast in the park. Then we went swimming for the rest of the day.

There was a girl there who was beautiful, and she knew it. She laid around on a towel all day to get a suntan. All the guys couldn't stop staring at her. We all wanted to date her, but she liked older guys. I ran into her years later and she had skin cancer all over her body. She told me about how she regretted all those hours she had spent in the sun. She passed away shortly after.

One day a friend of mine and I were riding a bike down a busy street headed to the park. It was one of those bikes with a banana seat, and I was sitting on the back. There was no sidewalk, so we were riding beside the curb and peddling fast.

Not sure why, but the car behind us didn't like us being on the road. Instead of going around, he ran over us. He floored the gas, rammed the back of the bike and we went airborne. I flew over my buddy and hit the ground first. The bike landed on me and he landed on the bike. We eventually got back up and made it to the park. We weren't hurt too seriously, but I remember it hurt a lot.

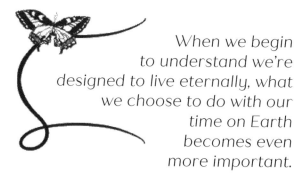

When we begin to understand we're designed to live eternally, what we choose to do with our time on Earth becomes even more important.

Some lessons from this little story: 1) enjoy your youth and have fun with your friends; 2) be generous to others but don't steal to make it happen; 3) take good care of yourself because you're not made to live on earth forever; 4) something may hurt but you'll probably survive it.

You'll find that how well you survive the things that happen to you is largely determined by how you choose to respond to those things. When we begin to understand we aren't designed to live on earth forever, the time we have on earth becomes more valuable. When we begin to understand we're designed to live eternally, what we choose to do with our time on earth becomes even more important. Give that some thought. It's worth your time.

THE LAWNMOWER SHOP

"Behold, I stand at the door and knock.
If anyone hears My voice and opens the
door, I will come in to him and dine with
him, and he with Me."
REV. 3:20

MY SISTER AND HER HUSBAND owned a lawnmower shop for a while, and I did some work for them as a kid. She taught me how to work on the mowers since I didn't really know anything about them. Customers would bring in their mowers for repairs and we always told them they needed a tune up.

Most of the time, all they needed was a key pin in the flywheel. Sometimes they needed points and condenser. Five cents might be all it took for the repair, but they were charged the price of a tune up every time. They had customers that did lawn work for a living, and we repaired all their stuff.

They had two big dogs in a cage out back for security: a Doberman and a Bulldog. It was too bad for anyone who tried to get in that fenced area to steal something. These dogs could eat them for dinner. My sister fed the dogs chicken.

You should never feed a dog chicken because the bones get stuck in their neck. I know because those dogs had them poking out of their neck like a spiked collar.

They would also feed them gunpowder just to make them meaner. Sometimes their employees were afraid to go back there because the dogs would bite.

Man, these dogs were mean but eventually they let me play with them. I had a go-cart, and we worked on the engine to make it really fast. When you took off across the gravel, it flew like a rocket. Those dogs didn't like the loud motor so they would bite the back tire with their teeth while the tires were spinning and drag me backward. Rocks flew everywhere.

My sister kept several guns and rifles behind the counter for protection. The shop was in a bad area, but she also wanted weapons because it was a fence shop for stolen goods. These guys would come in with stolen office equipment and other stuff. My sister bought their stuff cheap and then sold it for more money.

They began to do so much in stolen goods that they didn't get a lot of mowers fixed. These big dudes would come in complaining, and my sister would pull out a sawed-off shotgun. She would tell them to get out of her shop before she blew their brains out, and they would leave.

My sister didn't take anything off of anybody. She was tough and stood her ground, but she had a huge heart too. She was about ten years older than us, so she tried to look out for her younger brothers some while we were growing up.

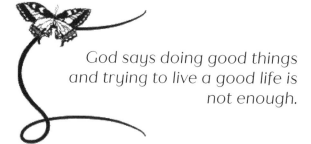

God says doing good things and trying to live a good life is not enough.

There were times when it seemed like she was the only person who really cared about me. She passed away several years ago. I love and miss her dearly. We talked many times about her need for the Lord Jesus to be her Savior, so I hope to see her in heaven one day.

She knew God says doing good things and trying to live a good life is not enough. We need His forgiveness, and He freely provides that gift to anyone who asks. He's ready to make His home in your heart today. All He asks is that you open the door.

AT HOME IN THE BAR

*"For I know the thoughts that I think
toward you, says the LORD, thoughts of
peace and not of evil, to give you a future
and a hope. Then you will call upon Me
and go and pray to Me, and I will listen to
you. And you will seek Me and find Me,
when you search for Me with
all your heart."*
JEREMIAH 29:11-13

FROM THIS POINT ON, life got pretty tough. My parents started drinking when I was about six years old. It wasn't so bad at first. My dad would stop at a nearby club after work to have a drink before coming home. He came home a little late and then a little later, and soon he was coming home drunk.

My mom would get mad and go to the bar to get him. She started meeting him at the bar and then they started drinking there together. That's how it all started. They probably never intended for it to get as bad as it did or thought about how it might affect their kids. Most people don't really think about how they will end up when they start drinking or doing drugs.

By now, they were drinking pretty heavily. They started working in the bars they drank in and eventually managed the bars. We lived in the bars they managed.

We slept on top of pool tables and inside of the car in the parking lot. Some nights we slept at my sister's house and sometimes we were left with one of my parent's friends for the night. This had been our life for a few years now, so the bar had become home for me.

Remember the Beer House bar we talked about earlier? It was an old brick warehouse looking building with a high ceiling. My dad lowered the ceiling over the bar area by hanging ceiling tiles. He built about a dozen rooms in the back, and we lived in two of them.

Our rooms had ceiling tiles, but they didn't lower the ceiling over the rest of the warehouse. Instead, the ceiling in the back was left high and open. Those rooms only had walls and doors. That area was used for parties by customers who drank even more back there, and a lot of fights happened in those rooms.

Some of their parties were *private*, if you know what I mean, and sometimes there were more than just two people rolling around on beds in there. They got noisy. Now, without ceilings, you know those parties weren't really private. Everyone could hear anything going on behind those walls including the kids. It's no wonder we knew more than we should have known about things at a very young age.

There were several biker clubs that partied at the bar. They parked their bikes inside near the back. Sometimes I climbed up on their bikes and pretended to ride. I've loved being on a bike all of my life. Maybe this is where it began. There's something about feeling the wind on your face that makes you feel free while riding a bike.

Being on a bike was a way to escape the life we were living inside that bar, even if it was just pretend. It was in the bar that I started using drugs. They were another way to escape the realities of life. Marijuana, pretty popular in those days, was just the start. Mind expanding drugs like LSD followed.

We called it a lot of names: blue microdot, purple haze, blotter acid, orange sunshine, etc. It didn't really matter what it was called. All that mattered was that it could take me anywhere but there.

My search to be in another place probably began long before smoking pot though. Living in a bar means alcohol is pretty easy to come by for a kid. I claim to be an alcoholic by the fifth grade. I don't know if that's really true, but it is true I drank a lot during my elementary school years.

It wasn't unusual to have vodka and beer nuts for breakfast before going to school. If school was part of the plan for the day, that is. My school grades were consistently failing. They passed me along anyway up to the ninth grade when I quit going to school for good.

One of my elementary teachers wrote this note on my report card: *Ernie has not been at kindergarten often enough for me to intelligently evaluate his work.* That was a true statement. Some people remember their favorite teacher. I don't remember any of mine because I was rarely there.

Drug and alcohol abuse are still around today so there must be people out there searching for something different, just like I was. Sometimes we don't see the answer because our minds are closed or we're looking in the wrong place. I was searching but didn't know what to look for. It's hard to find what you don't know you're looking for. I was searching for peace, joy and happiness, but they weren't in the pill and beer bottles I was holding. They were in Jesus. I just didn't know who He was yet.

Third Quarter

Days Present _11_   Days Absent _2-3_   Date _3/23/2_

Emotional and social growth are aids to mental development.

Mental Development	
Your Child:	
Expresses ideas creatively when using materials—blocks, clay, crayons, scissors	S
Listens with understanding to others' ideas. Pays attention	S
Is gaining language skills. Can describe happenings, explain work, tell stories	S
Observes skillfully. Can interpret pictures	S
Emotional Development	
Is growing in independence and self-reliance	S
Controls his actions for the good of the group	S
Puts away materials without being reminded	S
Physical Development	
Uses large muscles well as in throwing, climbing	S
Responds to rhythmic activity, as in skipping, marching	S
Has good posture in sitting, standing, walking	S
Social Development	
Is willing to cooperate and play fairly	S
Is kind and courteous in his daily relation to others	S
Expresses his ideas freely and with confidence	S

Teacher's Comments: Ernie has not been at Kdg. often enough for me to intelligently evaluate his work

Parents' Signature _Mrs. Oscar Gohas_

Ernie's kindergarten progress report (about 1961) showing his teacher's handwritten note: "Ernie has not been at Kindergarten often enough for me to intelligently evaluate his work."

HOME IS NOT WHAT YOU THINK

*"When my father and my mother forsake
me, then the LORD will take care of me."
PSALM 27:10*

IT WAS IN THE BEER HOUSE BAR that my mother tried to kill me. Now, some kids feel that way about their mom when they get a spanking or their phone privileges are taken away, but my mom really did try to kill me and more than once. Remember, my parents weren't really in their right mind all the time. Maybe if her mental state had not been altered by alcohol some of this would not have happened. We'll never know, will we?

But if you're a parent reading this and your home life is beginning to sound a little too familiar, I hope you'll consider your life right now in this moment. Today is the day to change the path you're on and maybe prevent some of this for yourself and the ones you love.

The morning started when I got up and went to the bar to grab a soda and chips for breakfast. Mom came out of the kitchen. She was still drunk from the night before, and she was upset. She started complaining because I wasn't born a girl. She said she really wanted a girl and having me was a mistake. She said she had been disappointed with me since the day I was born, and she wished I was dead. Really? Sure, she was drunk, but is that something you tell your kid?

At first, it was easy to ignore her. After all, she was drunk so who knew how she really felt, but then she reached under the counter where they kept the riot gun. That was a sawed-off shotgun that belonged to a policeman friend who worked for them. It was there to control the fights that happened in the bar. She stuck that shotgun between my eyes, cocked the hammer and stared me down saying, *"I should blow your blankety-blank brains out."* Well, now that made me mad.

So, I told her to go ahead and called her some names that weren't too nice. It wasn't like my life was great anyhow so what did it matter if she pulled the trigger? Then my crazy mom did it. My own mother tried to shoot me in the head.

It was a good thing for me it wasn't loaded because it usually was. I grabbed the shotgun and threw it as far away from her as possible. It knocked over a stack of beer glasses and sent them flying everywhere. I left my home in the bar that day and didn't come back for a while.

I'm not sure exactly what my age was when this happened, but it was late elementary or possibly early junior high school. It wasn't my first time to leave home. The first time I ran away it was to a hiding place underneath the house we were living in.

There was a secret mission into the kitchen to hunt for food each time my parents left the house, and then it was back under the house to hide until they left again. This cycle continued for quite some time. They drank, and I did drugs. We fought. I would leave and come back.

Then it would start all over. Finally, one day my parents rented a duplex, and we moved out of the bar. It was an old, rundown place, but it was home. Dad got a job working construction. You might think life would get better but that wasn't so.

At about thirteen years old, my friend's dad hired us to do some construction work with him. He paid cash under the table because we were legally too young to employ. The job was cleaning tiles with acid, and some of the chemical was stored at our house. While working for him, some friends came in to visit from another town. We had to sleep in one bed in my room because that's all the space we had.

My parents came home late after drinking one night and something crazy went off in my mother's head. She came into the bedroom while we were all asleep and picked up a bottle of the acid that was by the door. She poured it right into the middle of the bed while we were sleeping.

One friend woke up right away, and he got the rest of us up. We all jumped up just in time to watch the acid eating away at the mattress. It ate the shirt right off the back of one of my friends. It was amazing none of us were burned by the chemical.

My friend had woken us up in time to prevent that. We ran out the door and found another place to stay until my friends returned home. Then I went back home to confront my parents about what happened. Why in the world would my mom do that? It didn't make any sense, but they didn't like being confronted.

My approach probably wasn't nice, so we argued. Dad got mad, slammed a glass coke bottle to break it and tried to hit me with it. His friends pulled him away from me before anyone got hurt. My parents said to leave home and this time it was for good.

When you think about home, you probably think of the place you lived when you grew up and the people who lived there with you. You might think of your hometown or the place you're from. It often brings a good feeling with happy memories, but it's not that way for everyone. Thoughts of my home do not bring good memories.

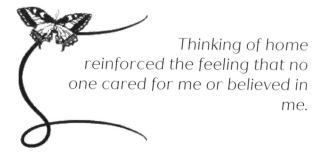

Thinking of home reinforced the feeling that no one cared for me or believed in me.

Instead, there are drunken faces and angry voices in my head. There are dirty houses, the kind you would probably call hoarder houses, complete with rats and roaches. There are beer brawls and police cars. My mom sitting on the sofa, drunk with cigarette smoke swirling around her head, while muttering nonsense to the invisible people in the room with her.

Thinking of home reinforced the feeling that no one cared for me or believed in me. Stupid was what they usually called me, and it was said so many times it seemed true.

My home life wasn't happy. I wasn't happy. Yet without understanding what hope was, my soul hoped for something better. Without knowing who God was, He was guiding me home to Himself, even through all of the bad stuff.

*Ernie, after removing his shirt on the day his
Mom threw acid on the bed that he was sleeping
in. This is the day she asked him to leave home
for good. He was about 13 years old!*

*Ernie at 14 years old and about the time he
dropped out of school.*

HOME IS A CIRCUS

"Keep me as the apple of Your eye;
Hide me under the shadow of Your wings."
PSALM 17:8

SOMETIME AFTER LEAVING home for good, a friend said it would be fun to join the circus. So, we went to the Oklahoma Fairground where the Ringling Bros. and Barnum & Bailey Circus was performing and asked to join their act. Since I was only about fourteen years old, the circus required a parent's consent to work.

They didn't want me at their house anyway, so it wasn't hard to get my parents to sign the papers. Soon it was time to board the circus train, and we were ready for a big adventure. Now, you probably think this is a joke, but it's not.

Life with the circus was lots of fun. We lived on a train, which was pretty cool, and traveled to a lot of places while performing. One of my uncles loved to hop trains from Oklahoma to Arkansas to bet on the races. He literally hopped onto the trains and never paid a fare.

I always enjoyed hearing him tell about his travels and couldn't wait to have some travel stories of my own to share with him. He was one of my favorite uncles, and it was going to be fun comparing rides with him. The circus gave me my own bunk on the train and a locker to put my stuff in.

Wow! Are you kidding? There was actually a bed to call my own there. It was just a train, but it felt like home to me. The people there looked out for me, and that was something new. The circus was the best thing ever!

My first job with the circus was as a prop man. Now, that's not anything like a circus clown. The prop man took care of the equipment needed for the circus acts. That job got old fast so next they let me work as a butcher.

You're probably thinking I was cutting up meat for dinner but that wasn't it at all. The circus butcher sold toys and balloons. That was the perfect job for me since it connected me with people, and I like to talk. The job paid pretty decent, and it didn't cost much to live on the train, so I felt like I had some money.

When we weren't performing, a ten-speed bike took me exploring around the town. It wasn't hard to learn my way around. Living on the streets taught me to be a quick learner. You have to learn fast when you're living on the streets or you won't survive long. And if you're not helping yourself, who else will? Well, other than God, but I couldn't see what He was doing for me yet.

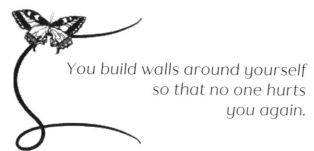

You build walls around yourself so that no one hurts you again.

You might think now that life included a bed, some cash and people looking out for me that it would make me want to stay put and enjoy the ride for a while, right? Settle down and make a new life? Well, for a short while it did, but the thing about being on the street is that you kind of get used to being there.

You build walls around yourself so that no one hurts you again. You don't really want anyone telling you what to do or when to do it either. Even though it was nice to have someone looking out for me, eventually it came back to doing the usual: Look for something new.

I didn't know it at the time, but Someone had been there looking out for me all along and that was the best thing that would ever happen to me.

HOME UNDERGROUND

*"If any of you lacks wisdom, let him ask of
God, who gives to all liberally and without
reproach, and it will be given to him."*
JAMES 1:5

AFTER LEAVING THE CIRCUS, it was time to be on my
own again. My next home would be an underground
tunnel below a busy street in Oklahoma City. The tunnel
was built as a crosswalk for the kids at an elementary
school to help keep them from getting run over as they
walked to and from school.

When the city built these tunnels years ago, they
probably never thought anyone would be living in them.
I wasn't much older than some of the kids going to this
school and should have been in school myself but that
wasn't happening. It was my choice and maybe not the
smartest decision. Later as an adult, there were
consequences caused by my limited education, but we
live and learn. My education was one built on street
smarts.

The kids who went to this school became good
buddies. Some of them packed extra food in their
lunches to share with me as they walked thru the tunnel
to the school. Some days brought a feast. Other days
brought starvation. It all depended on what happened
that day.

On the hungry days, there was the option to steal a meal or find one from a dumpster. Now don't say, *Eeewww*. Some of the food in there isn't as bad as you might think and for a starving kid, it's like having a home-cooked meal.

Except for nights when a friend might invite me to stay at his house, living in the crosswalk went on for several months. The crosswalk wasn't so bad. At first, concrete was my bed. It was cold and hard. Then I found an old, stained up mattress from a nursing home dumpster and put it in there. It was ugly, but it was warmer than concrete.

There was a water fountain to get a drink from and wash up in. It had a roof, so I was out of the weather. But it was hot in the summer and cold in the winter. It had bugs. It was dark every night and spooky.

So, when there was an offer to lay my head somewhere else, you know I took them up on it, especially during winter. Oklahoma gets cold. Even without attending school, I was smart enough to know not to freeze. See—street smarts.

After leaving the streets, getting an education became more important. The GED exam got the best of me twice before getting married. It seemed it wouldn't happen. At twenty-one years old, I could barely read.

The guy who led me to the Lord in 1974 played a record with someone reading the Bible and encouraged me to read along as he spoke. This did help but it still tried everyone's patience to hear me read during Bible study. It seemed like one sentence took forever. My wife helped a lot too.

A few years after we were married, my mother-in-law decided to get a GED. She had dropped out of school at sixteen to get married. My wife went with her to sign up for the test and she was supposed to sign me up for prep classes.

Well, she signed me up for the exam instead. Boy, was that upsetting. She said it would be good to test first because I might actually pass and, if it was a fail, we would know what to study.

Wouldn't you know there was a passing score at the end of that test? For some reason, my wife always believed in me. The lesson learned that day was that you never know what you can do until you try.

And, if at first you don't succeed, you really should try again. Those are often repeated but true statements. There were even a few college classes ahead for me after passing that test.

Back to the tunnels. Some cities have started closing tunnels like the one that was my home. They say these are areas where gang activities and crime take place. It's certain some bad things happen in these tunnels, but this one was there for me when it was needed.

That's something to be thankful for. Whatever your need is today, God already knows. He would love to talk with you about it. Just ask Him.

HOME UNDERGROUND

Entering the underground tunnel to the school crossing that Ernie called home for a while as a teenager. The kids left sack lunches for him on their way to classes some days.

Life inside the tunnel could be a little scary for a kid, especially in the dark.

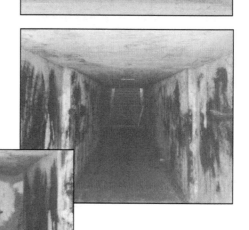

BELOW and RIGHT: Inside the tunnel where Ernie slept. The tunnel kept him out of the rain, but it was cold during Oklahoma winters. The tunnel did not have a light at night, but it did have plenty of bugs.

FRIENDS

"Greater love has no one than this,
than to lay down one's life for his friends."
JOHN 15:13

ALOT OF THE GOOD THINGS that happened to me as a street kid came from the friends who were there for me. There were times when a friend's parent cooked a good meal. Or let me sleep at their home for a night or two, maybe even a few. Get a shower and wash my clothes. Some of them even bought me new clothes.

There was one family who was especially good to me. We lost touch along the way and went many years not knowing what happened to each other. What a great thing it was to meet up with this friend and his family again years later, even though we were several states away from each other. It was a beautiful thing to finally be able to say thanks for caring.

Our family had a lot of issues, and this friend was always there to help. He listened to any problem I was willing to share with him. Like I said, you put a guard over your heart when it's been hurt, and you learn not to share everything.

How much they knew about how bad my circumstances really were, who knows? They just knew my home life wasn't good and that was enough. Sometimes I would be gone for a long time and just pop back into the scene again. It didn't matter. Their door was always open. They could be counted on to feed me or let me stay a few days if needed.

His mother treated me like one of her own. When you're not sure where you're going to lay your head from one day to the next, it feels good to know there is someone you can count on like this. So, when things got really bad, their house was usually where I headed.

He was a much better friend to me than I ever was to him. I know that now but didn't see it then. He always tried to keep me out of trouble, but it often happened that he would end up in trouble because of me instead.

One time we bought a bottle of whiskey and got lost while walking around drunk. I feel bad about all the trouble I got him into now. When my kids were trying to be a good influence on their own troubled friends, this friend always came to mind.

My kids often heard me tell them to be careful because what you choose to hang around is often what you become. There's a lot of truth to that, but I still thank God my kids had a heart to help others and that my friend was willing to try to help me.

BELIEVE there is GOOD in the WORLD. Be the Good!

My friend placed more importance on me than he did himself. To this day his friendship remains special to me. Although we don't see each other very much, he and his family are often in my thoughts because of what they did for me.

He's a big part of my life because of what he did for me. If it wasn't for friends like him and families like his, kids like me might not survive on the street. God must have special blessings reserved for this family because of the kindness they showed to people with needs.

There is a great quote posted on the wall of my grandson's school. It reads: "Believe **There** is **Good** in the world. **BE THE GOOD.**" Yes! Even after seeing so much bad, people like my friend confirm there is still good in this world. God, help me make the difference for someone who needs it today.

HOPE YOU CAN FORGIVE ME

"There is a way that seems right to a man,
But its end is the way of death."
PROVERBS 14:12

DID HE LIVE or did he die? God only knows the truth about what happened. See, we used to get into some really bad fights. Some were one-on-one fights. Some were gang fights. Sometimes my bad attitude would get the best of me and cause me to do things that weren't too smart.

I loved to fight and would fight just about anyone to be able to fight again. Their face was like a tomato to me and my fist was like a hammer used to smash it. Sometimes it worked; other times it hurt. They whipped me badly sometimes but that never stopped me from standing up to a fight.

When school districts started putting students on a bus from one school to another school across town, it caused a lot of gang fights. One time several gangs wanted to fight each other during a school football game. We met in the school parking lot after the game was over. People were still everywhere but we didn't care. We just wanted to fight.

There were fists, guns and knives. It was crazy. People got busted upside the head. Some were shot and some got stabbed.

One big guy jumped in front of me and pulled out a knife. He swung it at my face, so I blocked it with my left hand. His blade just about took off my left pointer finger. It scared me so much that I pulled out my stiletto. That's a knife where the blade comes right out from the front of the knife instead of the side.

It was razor sharp, too. It went into his side just above the left hip at the belt line and then my hand sank into his side pulling upward. The knife ripped him completely open and got stuck somewhere by his rib cage.

*It scared me—so I
ran and jumped into
a dumpster to hide.*

He opened up like a busted water bag and blood went everywhere. The knife was too slippery to pull out and got left inside him. His eyes were wide open with a shocked look on his face as he fell down with his insides spilling out.

It scared me—so I ran and jumped into a dumpster to hide. Climbing down deep into the bottom of the dumpster, I grabbed a bunch of paper and covered myself best as could be done. My hand was bleeding from where he had cut it so some of the paper was used to wrap my hand and help stop the bleeding.

Then it was time to lay quiet until the police and everyone else had left. When it seemed safe, I climbed out real slowly and walked to my parent's house to have them look at my hand. Mom gave me a washcloth and told me to wrap it around it until it was better.

The hand finally healed but I've often wondered what happened to the guy who got cut with my knife. If you're that guy and you're reading this, please forgive me. We were young and dumb. Yes, you cut me first, but it seemed your cut was the worst.

I hope and pray you survived and are doing okay today. God bless you wherever you may be and forgive me for all the pain my fighting caused.

HOME ON THE STREETS WAS SCARY

"I will both lie down in peace, and sleep;
For You alone, O LORD, make me
dwell in safety."
PSALM 4:8

FROM THE AGE OF THIRTEEN until joining the Army at eighteen years old, the streets of Oklahoma City were my home most of the time. Life as a street kid was scary. Sometimes my friends would let me stay at their houses. There was one really good friend who hung out with me on the streets a lot.

Sometimes I walked around all night while living on the streets just because there was nowhere to sleep.

We would stay out all night long just running the streets. We stole whiskey from the bar my parents ran and then walked the streets drinking it. Sometimes we liked to act like we had ran into a sign pole. We put our head close to the pole and pulled it back really fast while kicking the pole with the heel of our

71

boot. Then we fell to the ground holding our head and moaning like we were hurt.

One night when I did this, a lady stopped her car and got out to check on me. I thought it was funny and laughed my guts out at the prank. She didn't think it was funny though and started kicking me in the side.

We did some crazy things. We would yell at cars driving. Sometimes they would turn around to chase us. One night while drinking one of those big bottles of whiskey, we got lost in a weeping willow tree.

This tree was thick with limbs and leaves hanging all the way to the ground. We walked into the leaves and got lost. We were too drunk to find our way out. We ended up sleeping at the base of that tree until morning.

Sometimes I walked around all night while living on the streets just because there was nowhere to sleep. When cars drove by at night, I would hide in the bushes so people wouldn't see me. One night a guy hit me in the head with a lead pipe because he wanted to sleep in the corner of the sewer system where my stuff was at.

And there was that underground school crossing where crime was just waiting to happen. You never wanted to sleep too soundly on the street. My stomach got so hungry sometimes that I would go into a restaurant and put salt on a napkin just to have something to eat.

Clothes were hard to get for a kid living on the street, but it helped that a lot of people hung clothes on a line to dry back then. During the night, you could just go into somebody's backyard where there were clothes hanging out to dry on a clothesline and look for some that matched your size. You could take clean clothes off the line and hang your dirty ones up in exchange. Laundry was done. No more problem.

But one night an old man came outside with a gun asking who was there. I fell to the ground to hide and landed on a bunch of goathead stickers. That hurt!

When it rained, you couldn't find clothes on a line, but you could steal clothes from the dryers at laundromats. It was just easier to get caught and harder to find your size that way. But when you're a kid without a home or a job, you learn to do what you have to do to get the things you need. Hey, don't judge! After wearing the same clothes for a while, you need to change!

What I didn't know at the time was how much God loved me. Or that He could change me in ways I could never imagine if I only wanted. And that He wanted to provide everything that was needed for my life. What a difference it made in my life when I finally came to understand His plan for me.

We tend to think everything is up to us, but the truth is we're not as self-sufficient as we think we are. And the good thing about this truth is that we don't have to be. God is willing and able to be everything you need in your lifetime. You can depend on Him and trust His Word because He keeps His promises.

STEALING

"Let him who stole steal no longer, but rather let him labor, working with his hands what is good, that he may have something to give him who has need."
EPHESIANS 4:28

THERE ARE ONLY a few things that can be remembered from my childhood. Like when my oldest brother was beaten up in high school for growing his hair out long. Some of the school rednecks didn't like long hair so they got my brother cornered after school one day and knocked some teeth out of his head, literally. They gave him a free haircut, too. It was a lousy cut, but it was free. And it was short so he wouldn't need another one for a while.

Another memory is going to the mall with my friends. There was a Mexican food place there that we all liked to eat at. I rarely had money but liked to go with them anyway because they served free tortillas. They served them with butter or salsa and a glass of water for free. It didn't cost a dime, and it seemed like a great hot meal to me.

Every now and then one of my friends would share some of their leftovers or order a dinner for me. It was a great place to eat free, and it kept me off the street and out of the weather for a while. They even had a restroom where I could get cleaned up, too.

The mall had other free stuff, too. Well, really it was five-finger discount free. That's what we called stealing back then. One of my friends got arrested for shoplifting at the mall. The cops let me ride with them down to the station while he was being booked. They probably hoped tagging along might help keep me from trying the same thing in the future.

They were wrong. My friend was supposed to be a tough guy, but he didn't look so tough riding in that police car. He balled like a baby, and I had a good time laughing at him.

That never happened to me, but it may have been better if they had caught me. Stealing made me feel guilty at first. Later, the possibility of getting caught made me a little paranoid, but that didn't stop me from stealing. In fact, I stole even more and more as the years went by.

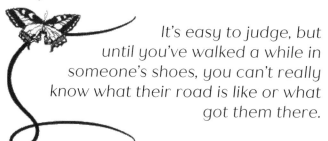

It's easy to judge, but until you've walked a while in someone's shoes, you can't really know what their road is like or what got them there.

My heart became hard and there was no reason to care. At first, only things needed to survive were stolen. Later, it was anything I wanted and without any conscience. Stealing became a way of life. I would steal from anyone including family and friends. Why not steal from my parents? It seemed like they were the reason I didn't have anything.

Living on the streets was tough as a kid, but it taught me a lot about life. My experiences helped me appreciate the things I had more later on in life. They helped me see people differently as well.

Knowing what put me on the streets as a kid and how it felt to live there is part of the reason I've spent so much time reaching out to the homeless as an adult. It's why I've tried to teach my family to love without judgment.

It's easy to judge, but until you've walked a while in someone's shoes, you can't really know what their road is like or what got them there. What we can know is that, in all circumstances, it's 'but for the grace of God, go I.'

We like to think we've earned what we have, and there's some truth to that. We should work and earn the things we enjoy in life. Stealing is wrong even if you're a kid trying to survive on the streets. But the greater truth is that anything we have on this earth is gained as a gracious gift of God.

We may not understand it all and we're sure to have some big questions about the fairness of life to ask God about when we're face to face with Him one day. I'm certain He won't mind our questions, and I know He'll have all the answers. Until then, this life will be better if we'll reach out to extend a 'hand-up' to those in need when we're able.

BURIED ALIVE

"A man's heart plans his way, but the
LORD directs his steps."
PROVERBS 16:9

BACK IN THE SEVENTIES, life was crazy. Anyone who lived during that time most likely has some memories to prove it. It was a time with a lot of drugs, drinking, partying and fighting. I tell people drugs are bad because of my experiences as an ex-drug user who did most anything out there.

You name it, and I did it: acid, pot, coke, speed, black mollies, cross tops, white crosses, reds, yellow jackets, uppers and downers, orange sunshine, LSD, STP, blue microdot, mescaline, and purple haze, just to name a few. I sniffed paint, lighter fluid, gasoline, Pam and lacquer thinner. I smoked hash, made rainbow salads, did crystal meth and more. But never heroin - so hooray for me.

My story started badly and could have ended badly, but it had a different ending thanks to God.

My wish is that I had never touched any of it. Drugs are a trap with an endless road to nowhere. The trip may last a few hours, but you end up addicted to whatever took you on the trip. It seems fun for a while. You think once or twice won't hurt, but before you know it, the drugs are controlling you instead of you controlling the drugs.

Eleven years old was too young to start doing drugs. By thirteen years, my drug use turned to drug sales for anyone who wanted them from third graders to adults, including some of my own family. Praise God for delivering me from that miserable life. He replaced all the bad things in my life with joy, peace and love.

My story started badly and could have ended badly, but it had a different ending thanks to God. There were so many drug trips taken during my life, and any of them could have killed me. This story is about a drug trip when my friends thought I died, and they buried me in the backyard.

On this day, we were throwing a party at a friend's house and everyone was either drunk or high. I was drinking heavily and smoking pot. A guy came in with a briefcase full of drugs, and I bought some orange sunshine from him. We liked orange sunshine because it was hallucinogenic.

We could do what was called a "seven-way hit" with it, which means we could cut it seven times so seven people could get high on one pill. But I swallowed it whole and began to die shortly after. Strange things were happening. Bugs were all over the table and wouldn't go away.

The counter had germs everywhere and the more we wiped, the more there were. Water came flowing out of the kitchen faucet like flowers. It was the drug, but it was driving me crazy.

There was a hamster in a cage in the living room. We would shotgun the hamster with pot and then watch him run upside down and backward in his cage. Have you ever gotten a hamster high? It was fun.

There was a guy watching a black light and listening to Pink Floyd's 2001 Space Odyssey Dark Side of the Moon. So, I sat down on a kitchen chair turned backwards with my arms on top of it and my chin on my arms and stared into the blacklight. Now that is not what you should do if you're on acid.

Suddenly, the guy was sitting in front of me with a blackhead on his face. Then they were all over his face. The blackheads started oozing and leaped out at me like long, black strings. It was creepy.

A guy came into the room laughing, and he wouldn't stop. I asked why he was laughing, and he said it was the lighter fluid. That was something new to me, so I naturally wanted to know more. He wanted to show me.

Now we were both sitting there huffing and snorting lighter fluid from a rag and laughing. You might think this sounds like it would be fun, but I'm telling you this to stop you from doing it. Some of my friends died from doing this. Don't ever try it. Not even once.

We loved it so much that when we ran out, we wanted more. So, we climbed into the car to get more beer and lighter fluid. It was the end of summer and kind of cool outside. The stars were shining bright and there was a light frost on the ground.

On the way to the store someone came up with the crazy idea to go swimming. There was a swimming hole nearby that all the bikers hung around during the summer. It was too cold to swim now so they had left. We were crazy though, so we decided to do it.

The swimming hole had a tree without limbs with a platform at the top. You could climb up the tree like a flagpole and jump off the platform into the pond. We climbed up to the top, and I sat down with my legs crossed. It was a thrill when you were high. The platform swayed all over the place. Everyone down below would yell for you to jump.

So, guess what? I jumped, but there was a small problem. I got stuck in mid-air and didn't fall down. I could see myself sitting in the air with my legs crossed and just stuck up there. It was really just my mind tripping on all the dope in my body, but it felt weird.

Then I started seeing myself going underwater, further and further down until my body was stuck on the bottom of the pond. Crud! What was happening? My cheeks were swelling up with air. My feet felt like they were wearing lead boots and wouldn't move. It seemed like I was going to die and none of my friends were helping.

Then suddenly my body shot up out of the water like a rocket. All that really happened was that my body went under the water and came back up, but my mind wasn't working right. I started swimming to shore but wasn't getting anywhere. No matter how fast my arms moved, my body was stuck in the middle of the pond. Then suddenly, it was laying on the shore. I didn't know how it happened, but that was the end of swimming for the night. I didn't want to die in that stupid pond.

Walking seemed like a better idea than swimming after that. Now remember I'm wasted and flying higher than a kite. It was still cold with frost all over the ground, yet I decided to lay in the grass and watch the stars. There were so many of them, and they were beautiful.

People started calling my name. They were saying it all long and drawn out, *Earn...ie..., Earn...ie..., Earn...ie...,* over and over again. It sounded cool so I started yelling my name, too.

Then a guy walked up and said my name: *"Ernie."*

"What-ee?" I answered.

He said: "Man, we're leaving. Let's go."

So, we left. Some went in the car. The rest of us walked. We decided to take a shortcut and walk down an alley. Well, it was kind of like an alley. It was a grass walkway with barbed wire fencing on each side. We came to a tall red brick wall with a large bubble at the top. We realized it was a pool, so we climbed the wall and went into the yard. Yeah, baby, and it was heated, too!

We jumped in and went down the slide into the warm water. Maybe no one was home, or at least they never called the police on us. We swam for a while and then went on to the store to catch up with everyone else.

Another shocking thing happened along the way. We crossed a college campus and walked right into the middle of a riot. Guns shooting and people fighting. Everyone took off running to get out of the line of fire except me.

I stood there tripping on the sound of the guns thinking, "Wow!" Something made me think it sounded cool. One of my friends grabbed me and said, "Run!" It made no sense to think it was so cool. It was deadly.

We finally made it to the store, and my friends asked how we were going to pay for the lighter fluid. Well, how do YOU think we were going to pay for it? My home was on the street. We had no money.

So, I picked up two cans of lighter fluid and walked right out of the store. Five-finger discount, right? No money? No problem!

When we left the store though, it seemed the traffic lights were working funny. Every time the light changed color, it exploded into a million different colors. It was weird so I rode in the back floorboard to keep the colors from hitting me.

On the way home, my friends decided to stop at a local club. We went inside and saw the club had giant spinning wheels on the walls. They covered the walls with different colors. Not a good place to be on acid, but we were there. The colors chased me all over the club.

I crawled under the pool tables to hide until we left. Yeah. You're probably wondering why those mind-expanding drugs seemed like fun, huh?

To my relief, we finally got home and were in a chair sniffing lighter fluid again. Instead of filtering it through a rag, I soaked the rag until fluid ran down my face and, even crazier, squirted it up my nose. The last thing I remember is having my head in a rag huffing when, all of a sudden, an orange Z appeared. It was on fire and buzzing.

It seemed like hours before that orange buzzing Z disappeared, and then there was total darkness. In my mind, it had only been a short while, but there were hours of orange sunshine left inside my body.

When my eyes adjusted to the darkness, I wished they hadn't. There was white silk a few inches from my face and white fringe surrounded me. It appeared to be a casket. Now remember, my friends were some crazy people. They were known to kill people and make them disappear so there were plenty of reasons to freak out.

Maybe I overdosed, and my friends decided to bury me out back so they wouldn't get in trouble for it. But what could be done to let them know I wasn't dead? Kicking and screaming seemed like the best idea. I just couldn't believe they would do this to me. I was still screaming for help when I suddenly came to. My jaw was sore, and there was a friend standing there.

He said they thought they had lost me to an overdose because my lips were turning purple, so he started slugging me, and it worked. Then I freaked out and started telling them to get off the drugs before they killed them. Guess who was huffing lighter fluid again the very next week? You guessed it.

Drugs are a never-ending trap. It's like one day you find out you're out of food in the icebox, so you go get high because you're out of food. Then when you come down from your high you find someone stole your icebox.

So, you go get high because someone stole your icebox. It's a trap, man. There's nothing good about it, I promise. It will catch up with you, and you will have problems. I was only about fourteen years old when this happened.

It would be another four years until someone would tell me about Jesus. There were so many other times that I should have been dead. If someone had not told me about Jesus, my story would have probably ended badly.

But God had better things planned, and He gave me life instead. Looking at my life today, it's hard to believe so much happened as a kid. My prayer for you is that you'll give God a chance. Jesus is real, drugs are fake, and you'll never find a better friend than Jesus.

FIGHT NIGHT

*"But you, O man of God, flee these things
and pursue righteousness,
godliness, faith, love, patience, gentleness.
Fight the good fight of faith,
lay hold on eternal life, to which you were
also called..."*
I TIMOTHY 6:11-12

ONE OF MY FRIENDS really loved trouble. Every time we were together, we ended up in some kind of fight. One day his little brother got into trouble for fighting at school and was sent to the principal's office. He got paddled and then sent home for a few days. My buddy didn't like that, so we headed up to the school to defend his little brother.

There were three of us: my buddy, myself and another friend. We all stood across the street from the school yelling for the principal to come off campus. We were planning to smash his head in with some chains my friend had brought. We knew we would be in trouble for trespassing if we did it on school property, so we stood across the street and yelled for him.

That sounds ridiculous now that we're older, but we weren't too worried about the trouble we would be in at the time. It kind of worked. He did come outside but he wouldn't come off the campus, so we didn't get to use the chains.

Since we couldn't get him to leave the school, we decided to head home. We started walking and put our thumbs out to hitch a ride. This Chevelle pulled over and opened its door. It drove off real fast when we started to get in, so we gave them the finger. They turned around so we decided to take our knives out and get ready in case they were looking for a fight.

When they came back around, they weren't looking for one. They said they were just kidding and told us to get in, so we did. They gave us a beer and started heading down the road. The driver said he needed to stop at a friend's house for a minute before they took us where we were going. To our surprise, they pulled into our neighborhood and stopped in front of my friend's girlfriend's house.

We all got out of the car and stood around drinking beer and talking. We were waiting for them to go knock on the door—but they didn't. Instead, the driver looked at my friend and asked what was on his pants. When he looked down at his pants, the guy planted a boot into his belly.

Well, it was on now. My friend took his knife out and tried to cut the driver. My knife got stuck in my pocket, so I jumped behind a tree. I came around the tree with my knife ready to use it but saw the guy was sitting on the trunk of the car laughing now. He said he had never seen anyone back his friend down like that before.

My friend had stuck the driver in the neck with his knife. It was just a little prick, but a little blood was running down his neck. His buddy thought it was so funny that he decided to just sit down and watch. He jumped off the car and handed me another beer. We shook hands and laughed.

Then they hopped into the car and left. My poor friend probably got the worst of it. He was still hurting from a good kick in the gut. He was getting plenty of attention from his girlfriend though, so it turned out okay for him too. We all just sat on the porch laughing about it and drinking our beer.

Somewhere out there, someone may be praying for you that you don't even know.

I don't know why fighting gave me such a thrill, but it did. There was a lot to learn about fighting spiritual battles after becoming a Christian. You may not know it, but there could be a battle going on in heaven concerning you right at this very moment.

Somewhere out there, someone may be praying for you that you don't even know. They may not know you but have heard about your situation from someone else. You've been in my prayers because I've prayed for everyone who reads this story.

It was my aunt who prayed for me. She lived far away so we didn't talk very much growing up. I didn't know about her prayers for me until my mom's death. That's when she told me she had been praying for me and my mom both for many years.

She was so happy to hear her prayers for me had been answered. She was there to pray with my mom before her death. She told me how my mom had expressed her love for the Lord to her before she died. It made me happy to hear my prayers for my mom had been answered too.

Fight the good fight of faith. Faith is your shield, and your sword is the Word of God. The battle is won on your knees. It's called spiritual warfare, and the win is eternal.

MY FIRST BIKER CUTS

"He has shown you, O man, what is good;
and what does the LORD require of you
but to do justly, to love mercy, and to walk
humbly with your God?"
MICAH 6:8

YOU KNOW, there are things you just forget about and sometimes it takes someone else to remind you of it again. My son reminded me of a story we talked about years ago. It was about my first set of biker cuts.

Today, motorcycle clubs can be for pleasure and considered kind of classy. There was nothing classy about the biker clubs of my younger days. Members were usually rough and the cuts they wore identified which club they belonged to. Cuts are jean jackets with the sleeves removed and patches sewn onto them. There was always a large patch on the middle of the back with their club name. This patch was called their colors.

There might be several smaller patches or pins on either side of the jacket too. Cuts were usually pretty dirty from being worn without washing. Some people say they're ugly, but I thought they were the coolest thing ever seen at the time.

I wanted some biker cuts to wear but was taught the only way to get them was to take them off of someone from another biker club. You had to rip their colors off and put yours on. That was pretty tough to do, even if you were tough.

As a kid living with bikers, I had seen a lot of biker fights. Today there was a big fight between two biker clubs on a bridge, and some other bikers were just sitting on the ends of the bridge watching the fight. A guy named Tiny was there with me. Now there were a lot of clubs with guys named Tiny, but they weren't usually very tiny at all. Most of them were about 300 pounds of pure meanness, just like this guy.

While sitting on a trike, a three-wheeled bike, watching the fight, Tiny said, "You've been wanting a set of cuts. Go take them off one of them but you have to rip their colors off before you put it on."

What? He knew those grown men were too big for a little guy like me to take cuts off of. He said he would blow one of those guys off his bike if I was willing to go over and take the cuts from him. We had a deal. Now these were big, mean bikers, and this fight was ugly.

I acted tough, or tried to, but the shaking was hard to control. Inside, I was really just a scared little kid. So, we stood there and Tiny shot the guy. He flew off the bike and landed on the bridge.

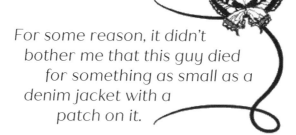

For some reason, it didn't bother me that this guy died for something as small as a denim jacket with a patch on it.

Then Tiny told me to go get the cuts. It made me a little nervous to think about what might happen if the guy wasn't dead. Tiny said to give him a kick and he would shoot him again if he moved. He didn't move when he was kicked so it was okay to take his cuts.

The colors wouldn't come off for me so Tiny ripped them off. Those biker cuts probably wouldn't have happened without a lot of help from Tiny, but I still felt like a real tough biker dude now.

For some reason, it didn't bother me that this guy died for something as small as a denim jacket with a patch on it. My heart was really turning to stone with all the meanness I was living around. You might feel your heart has been hardened by the things in your life too. Maybe you feel like there's no hope for someone like you.

Ernie wearing motorcycle cuts to the office as a Halloween costume

That's how it seemed to me, but years later someone would tell me about the One who died a death on a cross willingly to pay the debt I owed for all the bad things I had done. Could that really be? He changed my hardened heart with just a touch, and He wants to do the same for you.

Ernie with his motorcycle

MY SISTER'S KNIFE

"But God demonstrates His own love
toward us, in that while we were still
sinners, Christ died for us."
ROMANS 5:8

MY SISTER SHARED her home with me during the summer one year. She was older than me and lived in a trailer park with her boyfriend. He bought mobile homes, and they would fix them up to sell. They worked on them together to replace carpet, tile or whatever other repairs needed to be done to sell them.

After the repairs were done, my sister and one of her friends cleaned the trailers and then they were put up for sale. I was helping them with the repairs while I stayed with them that summer. One day we decided to take a break from laying carpet in one of the mobile homes. We were eating lunch, and my sister was sitting by the front door.

All of a sudden, her boyfriend's ex-wife opened the door. She pulled out a big knife and stabbed my sister in the right shoulder blade. The knife went all the way through her shoulder and into the wall.

Now my sister was a tough girl, and you know she was mad! She pulled that knife out of her shoulder and chased the woman around the trailer park trying to stab her back. The woman jumped into her car and drove away before my sister could catch her. We took my sister to the emergency room to get stitched up, but her shoulder was okay.

On another day, that same ex-wife came by and shot my sister's boyfriend in the face with a 22. Can't remember if it was a pistol or a rifle, but it didn't matter. It had a bullet that went into his chin, traveled down his arm and came out his elbow.

I don't think the ex-wife liked my sister or her ex-husband too much. We always kept an eye out for her after that, just in case she showed up again. It gave a little extra meaning to the saying, 'looking over your shoulder' for all of us. Times were interesting at their house. They weren't one bit boring at all!

My sister and I talked many times about the importance of making sure there would be a home for her in heaven when she died. Maybe this story will help you see the urgency of that too.

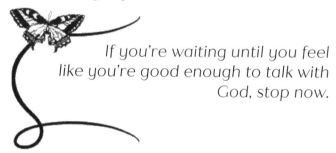

If you're waiting until you feel like you're good enough to talk with God, stop now.

The devil loves to tell people to wait one more day before making peace with God, but none of us are promised tomorrow. Waiting for the next chance to make peace with God isn't advisable for anyone since none of us are guaranteed we'll have that chance.

If you're waiting until you feel like you're good enough to talk with God, stop now. You'll never be that good, but God is. He loves you, and He wants you just as you are right now.

STEALING AND DRUGS

"My times are in Your hand; deliver me
from the hand of my enemies,
And from those who persecute me."
PSALM 31:15

BACK IN THE 1970'S, a man who said he was a hitman for the mafia hired me to steal personal checkbooks out of cars for him. He paid me ten bucks for each one, and there were lots of them. He also let me live in his garage apartment without paying rent.

He lived in a huge house in front of the garage. He was nice until you crossed him. Then it became hunting season on that person. He had scars all over his body. He would leave for a few days and come back in a new Dodge Charger with a trunk full of drugs, guns and a large roll of money. How he got it no one asked, but there were suspicions.

His younger brother was always bragging about the things they did. They threw big parties with drugs, drinks and guns everywhere. My girlfriend came with me to a party at their house once.

We were leaning against a sink in the upstairs kitchen when we heard his younger brother start telling someone how to stab in a way that would cause pain. He was standing behind the older brother who had hired me while he talked. He took his knife out, held it in a pinch about an inch from the end and then stabbed his brother in the back with it. His brother just twitched and kept drinking his beer like nothing happened. The younger brother wiped the blood off, put the knife back in his pocket and walked away.

Then some of my other friends came walking up the stairs. They were talking about how the guy who hired me was treating my friend's sister. She was the guy's girlfriend. My friend was full-blood Indian and mean as could be.

When the guy came upstairs, he was greeted by my friend. My friend grabbed him by the shirt, punched him in the face and down the staircase he flew. My friend leaped from the top of the stairs to the bottom and beat the dog out of that guy. It took three or four of us to pull him off. It probably wasn't such a smart thing for my friend to beat that guy up, especially if he really was a hitman for the mafia.

One day my friend's sister was sitting on the porch drinking a beer. She looked like something was on her mind, so I asked her what was up. She said the guy had asked her to marry him, and she said yes. They didn't have a date set yet. We were still sitting there talking when the guy and his younger brother pulled up in a car.

When he saw us sitting on the porch steps, he ran back to his car and looked under the front seat for something. She told me to get out of there because he would shoot me. She didn't have to say it twice. Bullets started coming at me, so my little legs started running fast and jumping fences. The shots kept coming so my legs kept moving all the way to the other side of town. Why was he shooting?

A few days later, I went back to see if it was safe to come home. My eyes watched the windows of his house for a gun while walking up the driveway to my garage apartment. There weren't any so it seemed safe to go on into the apartment.

While using the toilet, someone started banging on the front door. He started yelling for me to let him inside or he would break the door down. Guess this smart guy couldn't figure out the door was unlocked. I pulled my pants up fast and ran to a window. It would only open halfway.

Fear is a powerful thing, but it can only control you if you allow it.

Thank goodness for a skinny body. My thin body crawled through it and jumped into the alley below landing on two trash cans. While running down the alley, bullets were buzzing past my head again.

Good grief! It was getting old being scared to death by this guy. There was still no explanation for why he was shooting at me, but it wasn't the time to stop and ask either.

Two weeks later, a friend and his dad took me back to pick up my belongings and get out of there before he killed me. We started walking the long driveway to the back of the house while watching windows for a shotgun again. We didn't see one, so we went up the stairway and found the door was still open. My belongings were put into a bag quickly. It wasn't much.

Outside, my friend, his dad, the guy, and a police officer were all standing there. He could have killed us all and not lost any sleep over it, so it was scary walking down the steps toward him even though the policeman was there. The guy walked over to me and said if he ever saw me again, he would kill me. The Oklahoma City police officer asked if I wanted to have him arrested for the threat, but I said no. I didn't want to make him any madder!

Fear is a powerful thing, but it can only control you if you allow it. Placing your safety in the hands of a powerful God is a better option. He will always have your back, and you can trust Him.

NO WAY TO TREAT A FRIEND

*"Therefore, if anyone is in Christ, he is a
new creation; old things have passed away;
behold, all things have become new."*
2 CORINTHIANS 5:17

ONE FRIEND'S MOM let me stay with them at their house a few times. He was a good friend, but we did drugs together. He had long hair that he wore parted down the side most of the time instead of down the middle like everyone else. He was kind of a loner at parties. He just sat and listened to everyone else unless he was stoned.

Then he got a little more involved. We liked to experiment with drugs. We liked pot and acid, but we did mescaline most of the time. Mescaline causes hallucinations so we could have some fun with that. We would get high and then sit across from each other and try to blow each other's minds by making faces or screaming just to change the mood we were in. We used to stare at each other until our faces would melt into our laps.

Then we would try to pick our melted faces up and put them back onto each other's skulls, but his face would drip between my fingers back onto his lap instead. Sometimes we couldn't handle it. It seemed so real we weren't sure if it was really just the drugs we were on. Drug trips can get pretty weird.

Sometimes we overdid it and wondered if we would ever come down from the high we were on. I believe part of the reason we came down off these highs without harm is because someone like my uncle was praying for us.

My family went to visit him years later, and he told me how much it upset him when he heard about my living on the streets. He said that he had went hunting the streets for me. He wanted to adopt me but couldn't find me, so he asked God to keep me safe.

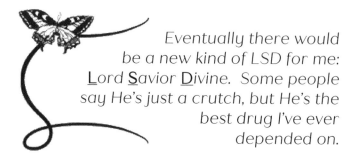

Eventually there would be a new kind of LSD for me: Lord Savior Divine. Some people say He's just a crutch, but He's the best drug I've ever depended on.

By the time he was looking for me, there was a pretty hateful, rebellious attitude growing inside of me so who knows if it would have worked out even if he had been able to get me off the streets. It's still good to know someone cared.

My buddy and his mom were fine people and they tried to help by letting me stay with them some. When his mom went off to work and my friend headed out to school, they left me in the house alone. They trusted me and that was a mistake.

While they were away, every drawer in the apartment would be gone through to see what could be stolen and sold to make a buck or two. Why would a person want to steal from a good friend who would cut his right arm off for you? They had money, food and a roof over their head. They looked like there were doing okay and probably wouldn't even miss those things.

It was about survival for me, so it seemed okay, but that was no way to treat a friend. Today I know that and wish it hadn't happened. Maybe someday my friend and his mom can forgive me for how poorly their kindness was paid back.

The money from selling stolen things was usually used to buy drugs. My favorite kind of drugs were ones that made you see things, like LSD. These drugs took me to a place where being homeless didn't matter anymore. They changed me but not for the better.

Eventually there would be a new kind of LSD for me: Lord Savior Divine. Some people say He's just a crutch, but He's the best drug I've ever depended on. He changed me, and He made everything better.

GHOSTS FROM THE PAST

*"Do not remember the former things,
Nor consider the things of old. Behold, I
will do a new thing; Now it shall spring
forth; shall you not know it? I will even
make a road in the wilderness and rivers in
the desert."*
ISAIAH 43:18-19

WHEN I WAS ABOUT FOURTEEN, there was a friend who lived with his mom and three brothers. He said their dad had left the family to join a biker club. That left the job of raising the younger brothers to my friend and his mom. God bless his mom and all the single moms out there for all they do to raise their children by themselves. It's a tough job, especially with kids like we were. We were such good buddies at the time that it seemed like we would be friends for life, but it didn't end that way.

We both dropped out of school sometime during the ninth grade, so we had plenty of time to hang out. Neither of us really cared much about school stuff but the other things my friend was into were pretty cool, mostly partying and drugs. He liked to fight, too. When we fought, we fought hard. We stuck up for each other and would probably have killed for each other if it came down to it.

Oh, by the way, this is the same friend who tried to beat up the principal for kicking his brother out of school. Remember him?

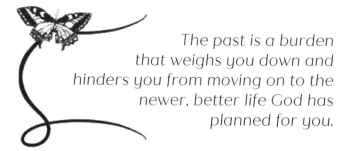

The past is a burden that weighs you down and hinders you from moving on to the newer, better life God has planned for you.

One day my friend was hanging out with another one of his friends. They were both a few years older than me, so I was a tagalong that day. That was probably good because the police liked to give them both a hard time. These guys would be walking down the street, and the police would pull over to search them every time they saw them.

For some reason, they didn't like my friend too much, and he usually ended up getting beat up whenever the police were around him. We would get him up and take him back home after they were done with him.

On this day we were riding around drinking beer and doing a drug called purple haze. They only had two hits. Since I was the youngest, they left me out this time. The trip went bad for my friends. Maybe it was bad dope, but they were really sick. They couldn't drive so it was my turn to take the wheel. At just 35 miles per hour, they would tell me to slow down. Then they told me to speed up.

No matter what I did, they got mad at me. Forget that! I decided to take them to his mom's house and park the car so they would stop complaining. When we got there, the other guy went to the bathroom barfing. My friend sat down in a recliner with his mind not right at all. His mom was there trying to help, but she was still drunk from the night before. Most of my friend's parents either drank or did drugs. She put on a pot of coffee thinking that might help. Actually, we all looked pretty bad.

Now you have to picture this in your mind. We're in an old house with a gas stove. She had an old metal coffee pot with no handle. It was mainly used for heating water to make instant coffee. We were in a hurry to get coffee into my friend to try to bring him down off the high, so the flames were turned way up on the stove.

My friend started walking around saying, "Coffee, coffee, coffee." He said it over and over again. He went over to the stove while the flames were blazing up around the pot and the water was boiling like crazy. He grabbed the pot with his bare hand. He had four fingers inside the pot and his thumb on the outside of it. He picked it up off the stove, and you could hear his fingers sizzling as they stuck to the hot metal.

His mom got the pot away from him and wrapped his hand with a towel. She took him back to the recliner. He just sat there mumbling random words. His mind was drifting further and further away, and he didn't even seem to notice his hand.

After a while he asked me to talk to him, so we started talking. Then he would tell me to shut up. Either way, he was mad. So, I left him and went to check on the other guy who was still in the bathroom throwing up. Suddenly, my friend appeared like a wild man and grabbed me by the throat. He had me up against the wall and raised a few inches off the floor using only one hand.

His mom came running to try to get him off of me before I choked to death. She finally succeeded and guided him back to the recliner. While sitting at the kitchen table trying to catch my breath, he came back and attacked me again. This time he had a knife and said he was going to kill me.

Well, that was enough. I ran to my parent's house and hid under a bed for the rest of the night so he wouldn't find me. His mom knocked on the door the next morning. It didn't seem like he was with her, so we opened the door. His mom said he had completely flipped out during the night, and she asked me to help.

There was no way that was going to happen. He had already tried to kill me twice, and he wasn't going to get another chance. But she said he was harmless and still all spaced out on the sofa. He wasn't talking anymore, and he hadn't slept all night. She kept insisting—so I gave in.

She was right. He had completely lost reality and was just staring into space. This went on for two days, and then he just snapped out of it. It worried me that he might come at me again, but he didn't remember anything.

The cops finally caught up with my friend one day and put him in prison. Don't remember what they hung him for, but you can bet the drugs didn't help. He heard a rumor that me and his girlfriend were fooling around while he was locked up. There wasn't any truth to it. He shouldn't have believed it, but he did.

Sitting in a prison cell can make you think things like that. That's why our friendship didn't end like we thought it would. He wrote me a letter when he heard the rumor about his girl. The letter haunted me for a lot of years. It had a drawing of a heart with a knife in it and said he was going to kill me when he got out.

Now, you tell something like that to a boy when he's about fourteen years old and the threat will scare him. It scared me. This guy would make good on his threat. So, for a long time after that, you would see me jump whenever someone walked up on me from behind. How long would it take until he found me? That question followed me into my adult years.

Then one day I realized the Bible says: *For to me, to live is Christ, and to die is gain.* (Philippians 1:21) That meant there was no reason to live in fear of my friend or any other shadow from my past any longer. Jesus had set me free from my past so I shouldn't be held back by the things that happened there anymore.

The past is a burden that weighs you down and hinders you from moving on to the newer, better life God has planned for you. Finally, my chains were removed, and my past was now in the past.

THUMBING THRU ARKANSAS

*"For I will be merciful to their
unrighteousness, and their sins
and their lawless deeds I will remember
no more."*
HEBREWS 8:12

HITCHHIKING ALL OVER the United States was a favorite way to get away from life in Oklahoma. Before taking off on one of these trips, I worked for a head shop that sold smoke items like water pipes, bongs and pinch pipes. They hired me to sell stuff for them because of my contacts with drug addicts and potheads. Working for them was to my advantage because it was an easy way to make a little cash, and it came with a few extra recreational benefits for me, too.

A friend of mine used to live in a town called Van Buren, Arkansas. He wanted to go back home to see his family, and we thought we might sell some water pipes and bongs for the shop while we were there. We hit the highway, thumbing it from Oklahoma City down Interstate 40.

We did real good catching rides until we were almost there. We had just caught a ride with some guy and loaded all our paraphernalia into his trunk when the guy took off. So much for selling our stuff along the way.

111

Shortly after he took off, we got stopped by the cops so maybe it was best we didn't have all that stuff on us at the time. Apparently, it was illegal to hitchhike on the Interstate, so we were arrested. We figured out really quick that the local cops didn't care much for long-haired hippies. They split us up inside the jail and harassed us with questions.

Then they put us back together in a cell. They came around in a few minutes holding a small bag of pot and asked who it belonged to. Well, my hair was longer than my friend's, so you know who they wanted to hang most. But they weren't going to outsmart me. I asked which bag they found it in.

It really didn't matter which bag they said, my bag was going to be the other one. Before my friend could answer, I laughed and told them that bag belonged to my friend. My thinking was right because sure enough they walked away without doing anything to him.

They charged us both with a fifteen-dollar fine for pedestrian on the interstate, which we couldn't pay, so they locked us up and kept us in that cell for 28 days. They denied us a phone call, so no one knew we were holed up in this little jail the whole time we were there. They fed us beans and cornbread every day. We had mushy oatmeal in the morning for breakfast, but they didn't give us anything to drink.

Yeah, it didn't seem right to us either, but we were kids. We didn't know anything about rights. There was another kid in the cell next to us. I don't know how long he had been there, but it must have been a while because he was set up like home in his cell. They treated him a little better than us.

He got water and coffee to drink so he would sneak some to us thru a hole in the wall. Eventually, they let us call home and my friend's mom came to pick us up.

Now that's some amazing grace!

The funny thing about our time in that jail is that it was never on record to our knowledge. It was like it was just erased. It was probably just some under the table redneck law kind of thing, but it makes me think of how God just erases the penalty of sin for anyone who asks Him for forgiveness through His Son, Jesus.

It's just gone. In the blink of an eye. Like it never happened. Now that's some amazing grace!

LOST IN A SNOWSTORM

*"This is My commandment,
that you love one another as I have
loved you."*
JOHN 15:12

THANK GOD for firemen. They put out all kinds of fires: burning buildings, car fires, wildfires and house fires. This one was my fire, and he rescued me. See, I was off on one of my crazy whims to hitchhike across the country again. It was my first time to head north during winter and it had me lost in the snow.

Now, don't get me wrong. We had snow in Oklahoma but not this much. It was coming down so hard you couldn't see a thing. It was fall when my hike began. The weather was cool but still nice outside. There was never any thought given to what might be ahead before leaving, only about having fun. So now there was no coat to put on, and it was freezing.

Stuck in Minnesota in the middle of a snowstorm was not a good place to be. I had no idea where this place was but knew I needed to get back home and was trying to find a way. Now, think about my childhood. No one taught me to read maps or use a compass. No one took me to Boy Scout meetings to learn survival skills. Surviving on the streets of Oklahoma was one thing, but surviving a northern winter was something different. This boy was cold, lost and feeling pretty stupid.

It may have been a foolish decision to hitchhike across the country but that didn't mean I was stupid. My parents had called me stupid all my life. They said it so much it seemed like it was true. But after Mom died, my dad moved in with us for a while, and the time he spent with my family helped me understand that wasn't so.

You probably need to know my dad was deaf as a child. Deaf children were treated differently in his time. People called him stupid because he couldn't hear. It really wouldn't be fair to fault my dad too much because he was just repeating things he lived and learned as a child. It's actually sad he grew up that way.

My wife wasn't stupid though so when he began to call her stupid, it helped me see things differently. When she told me how stupid he made her feel, that monkey jumped right off my back. Stupidity wasn't the issue at all.

Not having an education is a lot different than being stupid. We should be careful about saying things that cause people to feel dumb, especially our children. They just might believe you. That's what happened to me.

Now, there were a lot of foolish decisions made in my lifetime, especially this one to take off hitchhiking across the country in the cold. But you can bet there was some educating about northern winters happening on this trip.

A guy in a car pulled over and rolled his window down. He said it was too cold to be walking and told me to get in out of the freezing weather. This could have been another foolish decision, but it was so cold I climbed in anyway. He asked where I was headed and where I was from. Just trying to get home to Oklahoma was my response, and he joked that my directions were a little off course.

We laughed and he invited me home to his house for a warm meal. He said his wife was cooking up a storm—a warm one. Get it?

So here we are off on another adventure. This guy and his family were good people. I don't remember what we had to eat but it had to be delicious to my starving belly. We sat around and talked after dinner, mostly about me.

Where was I from? What was I doing in Minnesota? (Oh, so that's where we were!?!) Where was I headed? It was pretty much a repeat of the same things said in the car.

He told me he was a fireman, which was cool. His son was a long-distance ski jumper. He would climb up a high ramp to slide down and jump for distance. He could jump a long way but had wiped out on his last jump and broke his leg. That ended his jumping for the rest of the winter. Someone should have told him to break a leg for luck because he needed it!

They offered to let me stay in their basement until the weather cleared up. There was a bed and a small bathroom with a shower there. The family said it was a great idea to stay since there was nowhere else for me to go. They ended up letting me stay all winter, which was fun.

Most of the time, we were inside playing pinball since his son had a broken leg. They had two pinball machines in the basement. We played outside in the snow some, too. They bought me a pair of gloves, rubber boots and a coat.

We had a blast pulling each other around the block on a tire tube tied to the back of their pickup truck. Minnesota is called the Land of Ten Thousand Lakes, probably because it seems like there's a pond on every corner. Anyhow, we would fly around a corner on that tire tube, let go of the rope and slide over the hill onto a frozen pond.

Then there was another hill, and we'd do it all over again. Winter was so much fun there. We had snowball fights and everything. But winter turned into summer, and then it was time to leave. It was fun while it lasted.

They offered to buy me a bus ticket home, but it was warmer now and thumbing was free, so I said no. They said to keep the jacket and even gave me a few bucks for the road. It was hard leaving them, but it was time to split. They were the family I had always wished for and never had.

If you live in a nice home with three square meals a day, be thankful. Don't be foolish and throw it away. Learn from life or it can tear you apart with loneliness, emptiness, and bitterness, possibly for the rest of your life. Thank God for what you have at home, rules and all. This family will always be remembered with thankfulness for what they did for me, even though it may not have seemed that way to them at the time.

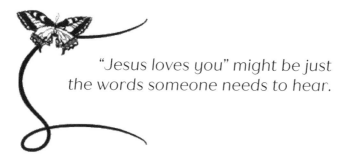

"Jesus loves you" might be just the words someone needs to hear.

There are many people from my past who don't have a story in this book. It would take a lifetime to tell you about them all, but I'm so thankful today for each one of them. Without their help, who knows where my life might have ended up?

A good bit of my time as a teenager was spent living on the streets. You could say the things that happened there were all my fault and that they were well deserved. That would probably be true in a lot of ways.

But you never know what road someone took to get where they're at in life unless you've walked that road with them. It's not always entirely their fault. Sometimes there's no one to blame at all. Sometimes even when it is their fault, it just takes one act of compassion to help put them back on a right path.

You never know until you try, and you might just be the one person who could make a difference for someone. The next time you see a young person in need and you're able to lend a hand *up*, please consider reaching out.

My kids have seen us take in many homeless people to stay for a while. Sometimes we could make a difference and other times we couldn't but, by God's grace, we tried where we could. It may only take a meal, a pair of shoes or a warm blanket. Be cautious about feeding their habits, but their tummy could sure use a meal and their heart could always use an encouraging word. *"Jesus loves you"* might be just the words someone needs to hear.

What an honor it is when they're able to see His face while looking at us. And what a blessing it becomes for us when we're able to see His face while looking at others.

A LIFE WASTED

*"...whereas you do not know what will
happen tomorrow. For what is your life?
It is even a vapor that appears for a little
time and then vanishes away."*
JAMES 4:14

THERE WAS A GOOD FRIEND who rode bikes with me. We were all-around best buddies, the kind that could fight and still hang out together. One day he and his girlfriend rode their bike to Louisiana and stopped at a bar along the way where they bought a hit of acid.

After they started riding again, the moon suddenly decided to park itself on the road in front of them. My friend reacted by trying to go around it, but he hit a tree head-on crushing the bike they were riding. He was tossed from the bike. She hit her head on the tree. It killed her but he survived.

The accident drove him crazy. Doctors couldn't help so his mother moved him into the garage by her house. He was an addict, so she didn't want him living inside the house with her.

She painted the room gray and put a rollaway bed and a little stove in there to keep him warm. The strangest thing she did was put a cardboard mailbox in there. She wrote U.S. MAIL on it, so he thought it was real. He wrote letters to his dead girlfriend every day and put them in the box for her. His mom took the letters out and put them in the trash every day.

He was so wasted all the time that he didn't know what was going on. He had me hit him up with heroin every day. We heated up the spoon and needle and shot him in his arm so he could function.

After a while, I had trouble finding a good vein to use anywhere. He would get mad at me. Sometimes he yelled and screamed so loud his mother would come to the garage and hit him up because I couldn't find the vein.

He had biker stuff all over the room. Posters, chains and skulls were hanging everywhere. It looked really cool. He had the rollaway. My bed was an old mattress on the floor across from his. It had a sheet on it that never got washed. He would throw knives at the wall above my head while he was high. That scared me at first, but he was good at it.

Sometimes we stole bicycles. We would cut off the front forks and extend them way out front to make it feel like a chopper. We sold most of them and kept one for us to ride.

Since I was staying with him, it was my job to get food for us. The bicycle made a quick getaway for me when stealing food from the store. If I couldn't get food from a store, then there were leftovers from a dumpster at a restaurant around the corner.

Sometimes the dumpster food actually tasted better than the food we cooked from the store. Sometimes his mom brought us food. When he felt good enough to go out at night, we would break into places and steal stuff to sell. Most of the time, he just stayed home and got high.

One night his mom and the fire department were there when I got back. Smoke was everywhere. He had caught himself on fire somehow and burned the garage down. My friend was no more. Maybe the little stove got knocked over and caught on fire. No one ever said what caused it. There was nowhere for me to go now except back onto the streets.

Life is short, and we don't know what tomorrow will bring. My friend didn't get to make a better tomorrow for himself. His was a life wasted. Someone once shared a poem about life with me that I love. I carry a copy to share with others whenever there's a chance. It's shared in part with you here to stress the importance of your life:

THE CLOCK OF LIFE

By Robert H. Smith

The clock of life is wound but once
And no one has the power
To tell just when the hands will stop
At late or early hour
To lose one's wealth is sad indeed
To lose one's health is more
But to lose a soul is such a loss
That no man can restore...

I've been told that thirty-nine people will die while you read this poem. I don't know if that's a true fact, but it's true that you or I could be next. Now is the time to make the choice that defines your future and decides your eternity. Choose wisely and make today count.

123

CAREY PLACE

*"For God has not given us a spirit of fear,
but of power and of love and of a
sound mind."*
2 TIMOTHY 1:7

SOME OF YOU older people may remember the seventies with tie dye shirts, bell bottom jeans and guys wearing long hair. Peace signs and make love, not war protests. Fast cars, drugs and other things.

It's all there in my past and maybe yours too. The long hair, the drinking, the drugs and the hitchhiking all over the USA. Out of everywhere my travels took me, there was one place that really sticks out. It was a creepy place, and it was right there in my hometown.

Everyone called this place "Carey's Place." There were rumors that a little girl was killed and buried in one of the yards there. It was never proven and probably just some kind of urban legend.

Some say the place is haunted though. It's part of Oklahoma City's historic district today. It was a neighborhood only two or three blocks long. It looked like there may have been gates on each end at one time, but the gates are no longer there.

Houses were two or three stories high, and it looked like a scene from The Twilight Zone. My friends joked that they thought it must have been used as a mental institution when the gates were in place.

In my day, dopers got high and went there to trip out while watching these people. It was crazy popular and bumper-to-bumper with cars at night. You drove through the streets moving maybe a half mile an hour because there were so many cars.

If you stopped, it caused all the cars behind you to stop. That was scary because people would go crazy and bang on the car and scream at you. They would jump on your car and ride on the hood. None of us were ever brave enough to get out of our cars. There were people on rooftops jumping rope at three in the morning, and people on porches acting crazy too. Even though it scared us, we would go around the block and drive through over and over again.

Carey's Place made for a great trip when you were stoned. It was fun and scary at the same time. Going back now, it doesn't seem so scary. There's nothing crazy like that going on at all. It doesn't make much sense why we liked going there so much since it frightened us, but we were just always glad the people never tried to get in the car with us.

We liked scary things like Carey's Place. That's why we played around with the Ouija board some too. That was pretty popular back in the 1970's. One night the board told us we were talking to Blackbeard's Ghost.

Next it said we were talking to my previous self and his name was Ernest Kenneth Hughes. He said his father had killed him. The funny thing about that is my dad busted through the door and tried to stab me with a knife that same night.

I don't recommend messing around with this evil spirit stuff. While it was amusing back then, today I know the spirit realm is real. There's only one spirit worth your time, and that is God's Holy Spirit.

In Galatians 5:22, the Bible says our time with Him brings love, joy, peace, patience, kindness, goodness, faithfulness, gentleness, and self-control. If these are the things you want in your life, it begins with having a talk with the right Spirit.

The sign at Carey Place in Oklahoma City's
Historic District

LOVE BROKE THRU

*"You will show me the path of life; in Your
presence is fullness of joy; at Your right
hand are pleasures forevermore."*
PSALM 16:11

LET ME TELL YOU A STORY about how God changed
me from who I was then to who I am today. It's a story
about how His love delivered me and turned my life
around. Have wrongs been done since that day? Sure.

You'll never hear me claim to be perfect. But my
wrongs *(God calls these sins)* have been made right
because of what Jesus did for me *(God calls this
forgiveness)*. If you were wronged by me in the past, I'm
sorry and hope you'll forgive me.

This story begins when my brother joined the Army
and asked me to come see him. He was stationed at Fort
Bragg, North Carolina. So, I bought a bus ticket and filled
my pockets with drugs to sell along the way to pay for
the rest of the trip.

It was a long ride on the bus. There was a guy on the
bus who was in the Army too. We sat together and talked
during the ride. When we pulled into the Little Rock
terminal, there was time to spare so it was a good chance
to sell drugs.

The Army guy found a girl to talk with while we were
stopped. He introduced me to the girl, and we all hung

out together. Now, girls talked a lot when they got high and that could get you arrested so they weren't usually who you liked to be around when you were carrying drugs.

This girl was cool though, so she seemed okay. When we got back on the bus, she pointed to a window seat and told me to sit there. Then she sat down beside me.

The Army guy got mad and went to the back of the bus. He wouldn't talk to me anymore that whole trip. When we got to Nashville, she got off and gave me her phone number.

We finally got to North Carolina and my brother met me at the bus station. Oh! Forgot to tell you this trip was for his wedding. We went to his house, and he put me up for about a month or so before the wedding.

One of my brother's Army buddies let me hang out with him. He was a short guy with a new Harley motorcycle, which made me happy. Better than that, he had drugs, so we drank and got wasted on chocolate mescaline together. The drug use bothered my brother.

Years later, he told me they switched some of my pills with birth control pills. For some reason, they thought that was funny. We rode his Harley all over town, but he couldn't reach the ground so his bike would fall over every time we stopped at a red light. It got old picking up his bike, so we went back to my brother's house.

Soon it was time for the wedding. We went back to my brother's house afterward, and his new wife didn't want to let me in. She said she didn't like me, and it was time for me to go.

My brother defended me. He told her he had invited me and maybe she should leave and come back when she could apologize. Now, my brother doesn't remember this story but it's in my memory. Maybe because it was important to me. It was a surprise that he took up for me.

While living on the streets, it felt like he abandoned me and that had caused me to resent him. It didn't occur to me that my brother was also a kid at the time and might have been living through his own set of issues from the crazy life we had.

So, on this day, it felt good to hear him taking up for me, and that memory stuck with me. It's true my mind was on drugs then so who knows. Even if the memory isn't good, I sure felt good about my brother that day.

But his wife was right. My welcome had been worn out, and it was time to go. As my brother drove me to the bus, he asked me to give up the drugs before they killed me. My response was that he should give up drinking instead. Then it was time to get on a bus headed home.

A funny thing happened then. As we pulled into the Nashville bus station, can you guess who was sitting on the sidewalk waiting on a bus to Little Rock? It was a month later, but there she was. She was as shocked as I was.

We got a seat at the back of the bus and took off to Little Rock. We were still hitting it off pretty good. She gave me her phone number again before getting off the bus, and this time I kept it. Then it was on to Oklahoma.

My brother finally talked me into joining the Army. Everyone else probably thought it would be a more stable home for me than the street. But I remembered doing drugs with my brother's Army buddy and thought it would be a good place to do more drugs. The Army also came with a bed of my own to chill out on, which would be nice.

Before leaving for basic training, some girls threw me a going away party. It was early 1974, and the country was winding down from the Vietnam War. But it seemed like maybe they thought I wouldn't return because they asked for a lock of hair to remember me by.

Now my hair was all the way down to my elbow, like most guys in the 70's. They did a really bad job of cutting my hair, so the barber got to cut it all off the next day. Somebody should have told me the Army was going to shave my head anyway.

Basic training was at Fort Polk, Louisiana. They called it "Little Vietnam." It was hot and humid with lots of snakes. They gave us uniforms and boots at the reception station. They taught us how to make a bed, put on the uniform and brush our teeth.

I don't remember owning a toothbrush of my own before joining the Army. They taught us how to polish boots like glass. Then they said we were ready for Basic Training. That's funny—we thought we were at Basic Training already!

They loaded us into cattle trucks with electric doors. When we got there, they opened the doors and started throwing us into a big ditch. The drill instructor yelled for us to get out of the ditch and into formation. We thought we had just stepped into hell.

While standing in a formation, we listened to them scream at us to pick up our duffle bag and throw it down. They repeated yelling at us to do it over and over again for hours. They wanted us to lift it up over our head.

After a while, we couldn't lift it even a few inches. It sure wasn't going over our heads anymore. Then there were push-ups and the inverted ladder. Then they fed us lunch. We got our food and sat down exhausted.

As soon as we sat down, they said it was time to go. We didn't get to take one bite. The food was stuffed into our pockets for later while they weren't looking. We learned to be at the front of the line. You never wanted to be at the end. Basic training was hard, but we hung in there.

It was really hot, and a heat stroke sent me to an Army hospital. We were marching as fast as we could on a speed march. Then we went to an asphalt parking lot to do marching drills and stood in formation for hours. I passed out.

My drill instructor (DI) took me to the barracks and threw me into a cold shower. There I was laying on the shower floor, shivering with a high fever, when the captain came in and asked what was going on.

The DI said, *"Sir, this soldier thinks he's having a heat stroke."*

The captain walked right into the shower wearing his dress uniform and felt my head. He picked me up, put me in his Chevy and rushed me to the hospital.

Fort Polk was no picnic. We had to go out into the swamps listening for a motor at night and find it in the dark. They told us if we saw a snake swimming by to be still and let him go. There were lots of snakes.

And spiders! I hate spiders! We slept outside with our sleeping bags zipped up tight, but it didn't help. When you unzipped in the morning, spiders came jumping out of that bag right along with you. They had vines that had three-inch thorns on them. We called them 'wait-a-minute' vines because they grabbed your clothes and said, *"Wait a minute!"*

You ran into them a lot in the middle of the dark night with no moonlight. One time, a vine grabbed me and caused me to drop my weapon into the swamp. It was no fun looking for it in the dirty water. We survived though and made it to graduation. As much as we hated our DI, we respected him when it was all said and done. He taught us how to survive.

Advanced Individual Training (AIT), where they train you for specialized skills was up next, but we couldn't leave for two weeks. They had us in the holdover barracks with nothing to do except drink and watch new recruits come in on the cattle trucks. They threw them into the ditches too.

Our DI went to the orderly room while the new group got into formation. We decided it would be funny to pull one over on him. One of the recruits was a big guy who looked like he might be a boxer. I told him to bust the DI in the mouth when he yelled at him and he would respect him for it.

I explained he was just trying to find out who had enough guts to stand up to him. He bought it, so it was time to go back to our table and wait for the show. This was going to be good. When the DI got in this guy's face yelling, he busted him in the jaw so hard it knocked him on his tail.

The DI got up off the ground, grabbed the guy and took him into the orderly room. That poor soldier had a busted lip and two black eyes when he came out. We just looked the other way. The DI came over and asked who put him up to that. All my buddies pointed at me, and the DI just laughed.

We shipped out to Fort Leonard Wood, Missouri, for AIT a few days later. Training started all over again, but this time there was a problem. No one got along. There were fights all the time, and our sergeant was nuts.

He would fight with his wife at home and then come shoot at our barracks using live rounds. It was a wonder someone didn't get killed. He made us low crawl through poison ivy so bad it caused one soldier to go temporarily blind.

They punished the sergeant by having him drive a trash truck for a while. Half the company went absent without leave (AWOL). We thought they were going to kill us for everyone going AWOL, but they brought in a new sergeant instead.

He lined us up and threatened we would have to report to him if anyone else went AWOL. They weren't too scared. Half the remaining guys left after that. The rest of us were sure they would kill us now.

They put us into formation the next day and said anyone who wanted out of the Army, or their MOS changed, should step out. They didn't have to ask me twice. They were crazy here, and this was my chance to escape. They looked at me like I had lost my mind. They sent me to talk to a shrink.

He wanted to know my reason for wanting to leave, so he heard about all the crazy stuff they did there. He tried to assure me those things weren't normal. I said he sure had that right! They gave me a full honorable discharge.

Who knows why they did that? Maybe they just had too many soldiers enlisted since we were no longer in Vietnam, but it didn't matter. All that mattered to me was getting out of there. Before leaving, my sergeant told me he had papers to send me to Thailand. I told him my red, white and blue eagle said to go home instead.

Since AIT was close to Arkansas, it seemed like a good idea to go see that girl in Little Rock on my way home. It had been almost a year since we were on that bus ride together, but she remembered me and was happy to hear from me when I called.

After getting a motel room downtown, I went to a jewelry store and decided to buy her the first thing I saw on the shelf. It was a cross necklace. She was excited about the gift and gave me a big hug. There was a poster of a long-haired guy with a beard and some kind of ring with thorns on his head hanging in her house.

The poster had one word printed at the bottom: Jesus. He wasn't familiar to me, but I thought maybe he was a new Spanish rock singer that came out during Basic or AIT. It wasn't really given much thought at the time.

My friend wanted me to meet her mom and some friends. Every house we went to had cool people. Some did drugs; some didn't. It was strange that she never wanted to do drugs with them though. Back in my room, there was whiskey.

See, I was a speed freak in the Army. I brought it from home to sell to the guys on base. The guys wanted it to help them stay awake during training, but the sales supported my own habit. We ate a ton of it. This girl had used before, but she didn't seem to be doing drugs or drinking at all anymore.

It had been almost a week now and going without drugs was making me shake. Money was running low, and there was dope available for me at home. When I told her it was time to leave, she didn't want me to go. She said her brother would let me stay at his place. That didn't sound like a good idea to me, but she took me to see him anyway.

Her brother ran a recreation center where people played foosball and pinball machines. He looked cool. He must have been into that new rock singer too, because the words *Trucking for Jesus* were on the back of his jean jacket. He was barefoot with blue jeans and had long hair.

My first thought was that he probably did drugs since he was into rock groups and had long hair. He was strange though because every time he scored a goal playing foosball he said, *"Praise the Lord!"* I had no idea what that meant, but he said it all the time. She asked him to let me stay with him a while and he agreed. I told him that I would steal his stuff, but he didn't care. This guy just loved me right into the kingdom of God.

He made a spot for me on a rollaway bed in the living room. He wasn't a doper, after all. He and his wife didn't smoke pot or even drink.

Life was really miserable, and my money was gone. My body had the shakes, what they called DT's, from addiction. There were no drugs without money. No one would give me a gun to end it all with either.

At the end of my ropes one night, I headed back to his house shakes and all. It was late, but the light was on. Her brother was waiting on the couch with a Bible in his hand. Just when it seemed this day couldn't get any worse, it looked like it might end with being kicked out on the streets again.

When the door opened, he said, *"Hey, brother."* Now, he always called me brother for some reason. Surely, he knew we didn't have the same mother! He told me to have a seat. Man, my body was really shaking now. He was about to say something that didn't go with my lifestyle, and this wasn't what I wanted to do right now.

His question surprised me. He said he thought we had talked about my being saved when we first met. Did we? Yes, we did. Suddenly, everything came spilling out to him.

Talking honestly with someone was something new to me, but it was like it had to happen. The first time that word had been used around me was in the Army. When we were in trouble, we could choose between kitchen patrol (KP) or church. We usually chose church because it was easier.

Some of the guys would go to the front to get saved before leaving, but it wasn't clear what they were getting saved from. I never understood it but admitted that's where I had heard about it.

Looking confused he said, *"You mean you didn't get saved?"* It would be hard to do something when you didn't know what it was, so the honest answer had to be "no." But you know he could already tell that by my actions, and that's why he was asking.

He read some Bible verses, explained salvation and introduced me to Jesus. So, it turns out that guy in the poster wasn't really a new rock singer after all. He had died on a cross to provide forgiveness for my sins.

Wow! Someone would do that for me? He asked if I wanted to accept Jesus as Lord of my life. That was a big question, but there wasn't any hesitation in my answer: *"If this is what changed your sister's life and gave her the kind of peace and happiness she has now, then this is what I want."*

I didn't even know how to pray so he helped me. My prayer went something like this: *"God, if you're real like this man says, please forgive me, and come into my heart and change me."*

This is why his sister was so excited about the cross necklace. Before that prayer, I wanted to die, just like on so many other nights before. My prayer was sincere and the desire for change was deep. Repentance was real for me, and my sins were forgiven. The words you pray don't matter nearly as much as what God hears from your heart. He understands you.

He doesn't care how bad you think you are or how long it's been since you've been to church.

God spoke to me after my prayer that night. Not audibly but clearly within my heart. He said, *"Ernie, you've given me your whole heart and held nothing back and so I've got hold of your heart and will never let you go."* At that moment, I felt Him reach in and touch my heart. I felt Him say, *"I've got you, son."*

That was October 2, 1974. That day wasn't about religion. It was about starting a relationship. He became a Father to me on that day, and He still holds my heart today. I stumble and fail Him sometimes.

He has been disappointed in me, but God is more loving and forgiving than any man. In Psalm 103, the Bible says He removes our sins "as far as the east is from the west," and He remembers them no more. That's love.

He is drawing me to write this book. It's His story, not mine. It's the story of how He saved me from myself. Hopefully, it will be more than just some story to read and be helpful to others. If that someone is you, then my prayer is that you'll be spared the hard lessons in life.

He doesn't care how bad you think you are or how long it's been since you've been to church. He doesn't care how long it's been since you prayed. Today is the day He wants to hear from you. He wants to release you from the things that are holding you down.

You may think you're tough. Maybe you're lonely and just need a friend. What's cool about God is that He's not pushy. He just asks and lets you decide. That tug you're feeling on your heart—that's all Him.

ABOVE: Ernie in Army dress uniform (left) and basic training uniform (right) in 1974; age 18 years.

BELOW: Ernie making fun of his brother's Army uniform; age about 16 years.

MY MOST MEANINGFUL CHRISTMAS

*"Who shall separate us from the love of
Christ?...For I am persuaded that neither
death nor life, nor angels nor principalities
nor powers, nor things present nor things
to come, nor height nor depth, nor any
other created thing, shall be able to
separate us from the love of God which is
in Christ Jesus our Lord."*
ROMANS 8:35-39

MANY FAMILIES ENJOY a big Christmas celebration together every year. My most special Christmas memory is the one when God showed me that there is love in this world. It was the Christmas of 1974. The man who had taken me off the streets into his home and led me to Jesus had a Christmas party at his house for his family. It was cold outside. The ground was covered with snow, and there were icicles on all the houses. It looked like a storybook.

Our family never had a real Christmas gathering that I can remember. We may have had one at some time, but it's not something in my memory. When the man who took me off the streets had this gathering at his home, it was awkward for me.

Family gatherings were new to me, and this wasn't my family, so it didn't feel like there was a place for me. A little depressed, I went outside alone to enjoy feeling sorry for myself. Thru the window, you could see everyone giving each other their gifts. It made me feel bad to know there wasn't a gift to give the one family that had helped me the most, so it seemed best to let them share their personal time together.

There was a large rock behind the garage with snow on it. I brushed it off and sat down with my jacket wrapped around me. It was lightly snowing out but not enough for me to have to go back into the house.

Sitting there trying to think of the last Christmas with my family, there was not even one to be remembered. My friend's mother walked up beside me with a package in her hand. She asked me to scoot over and let her sit down.

We brushed off some more snow to clean her a seat. She was concerned about me being out there by myself. She said, *"Why are you out here?"* like she could read my mind. Tears were in my eyes as we talked about my Christmas memories.

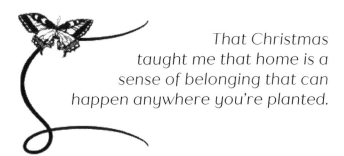

That Christmas taught me that home is a sense of belonging that can happen anywhere you're planted.

"I wish I had a family like this one," I confessed to her. *"One where people really love each other and show it. I want that kind of love. I've seen it in the past with some of my other friends and their families. They touched my heart, and*

I've always wanted to know what it would be like to have a family that loved me, even if it was just at Christmas."

She said, *"You have a family like that right here, Ernie. We all love you and want you to be a part of our family."*

Then the tears came spilling out. She hugged my neck and handed me the gift. She said it was a Christmas present from all of them. That light blue Levi denim shirt they gave me touched my heart so much. It was the best present ever received. There were so many tears while sitting out there on that rock. Then after the tears, we went into the house to enjoy our family Christmas dinner together.

That denim shirt is still in my closet over forty years later. There have been many more Christmas dinners with family since that day, so it doesn't fit anymore, but that doesn't matter. It means so much to me that it will always be kept.

For me, that Christmas was the beginning of learning how to love others and how to receive love. That Christmas taught me that home is a sense of belonging that can happen anywhere you're planted, that family can be much bigger than just the ones you're born to and that God can use anyone to touch a heart.

Thank you, God, for bringing me home to this family with such a big heart, for giving me such a wonderful Christmas that year and for all the wonderful Christmases since that one. True love really was born in a manger.

DON'T BE AFRAID
TO SPEAK UP

*"For God so loved the world that He gave
His only begotten Son,
that whoever believes in Him should not
perish but have everlasting life."*
JOHN 3:16

ONE DAY SHORTLY AFTER giving my heart to the Lord, I was sitting in the balcony of a church by myself. There were still a lot of things for me to figure out as a new Christian and how to trust people was one of them. Sometimes being alone helped to sort things out. God spoke to me while sitting there.

Again, not out loud but in my heart. He wanted me to truly see how happy my life had become because of what He had done for me. He began to show me some of the things from my past that I had forgotten about, and He reminded me that there was no more drug addiction in my life. No more desire for alcohol.

The hatred in my heart had disappeared, and my days were no longer filled with fighting. It was gone. All of it. God loved me and had changed my life so much. Tears ran down my face.

Never in my life were there so many tears. God was drawing on my heart to begin sharing how He had changed my life with others. He would lead and speak thru me if I would just be willing to follow Him. I would follow Him anywhere.

The next weekend someone invited me to a Christian coffeehouse in Little Rock. I didn't know what that was, but it sounded interesting. They had Bible study and a time for sharing.

Someone asked me to share about my salvation. I told them how my friend had led me to the Lord. They asked about my past and said it was amazing how God delivered me. They asked me to share my story with others.

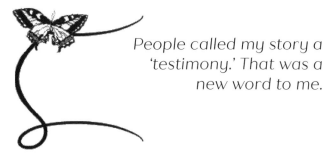

People called my story a 'testimony.' That was a new word to me.

So, from there came more opportunities to go from place to place sharing how God had changed my life. People called my story a *'testimony.'* That was a new word to me. To be honest, it really didn't make sense to me what people saw in my story. My life seemed normal to me. But people listened, and some people gave their hearts to God after hearing what He had done for me, so the stories continued.

Once, we went to a church somewhere in the woods in Arkansas to minister. The people with me played music and sang. Then it was my turn to speak. They heard God loved them and how He was crucified on a cross for their sins. They heard how He would have died for them even if they were the only person left on this earth.

He didn't especially want to do it because He had asked His *"Father, if it is Your will, take this cup away from me."*

(Luke 22:42) But Jesus loved His Father and wanted to do His will, so He did it.

See, the Bible says we are all born as sinners. Some of us have tempers. Some of us gossip, lie and steal. Others cheat on our spouses. The list goes on and on, but God sent His only Son to die for our sins. Now that seems pretty amazing to me. Why would anybody want to die for me? For some reason, He loved me enough to do it even though it wasn't deserved.

Some guys in the back of the church were making noise and throwing paper wads at us as we spoke. We just kept talking. After church, those guys were looking inside our car. One guy told the other one that he was going to take that nice coat laying in our back seat. The other guy said he was going to take the hubcaps, too.

Being outside and overhearing them, I walked over and told them they didn't have to steal those things. The leather jacket was a gift someone had given me. Now it was my gift to them. My hip knife popped the hubcaps off, and they got those, too. (Now, some of you are probably wondering what hubcaps are but your grandpa can explain!)

They walked away with their heads down. It shocked them. Back inside the church, my friends heard about what happened outside. They were shocked, too, especially the guy that owned the hubcaps. But these were just things, and something more important was taking place that night.

We were hungry so we wondered where we might get something to eat. As we were leaving, the guy who got my jacket pulled up. He asked where we were headed, and we told him we were looking for food. He told us to follow him, so we did. We drove for what seemed like forever.

The girls worried he might be taking us somewhere to do something bad to us. But then we pulled into a McDonalds. He pulled up next to us, and we offered to buy him a burger. He agreed to come in and sit with us for a minute.

HUH! That's what he thought, but God had a better idea. We went inside and sat in a booth after ordering our food. He got put in the middle between us. Oh, yeah!

We got to talking and he told us he burned his Bible because he didn't want it anymore. After talking a while, he admitted he hadn't burned it but had just hidden it in the top of his closet. We ended up leading him to the Lord right there in McDonalds. We gave him our phone number and stayed in touch for a while.

Eventually, we lost contact with him and don't know where he is anymore. But God always knows our heart, and He is always with us wherever we go. Isn't that good to know?

POTATOES FROM HEAVEN

"But as for you, you meant evil against me;
but God meant it for good, in order to
bring it about as it is this day..."
GENESIS 50: 20

THERE ARE SOME PEOPLE who just don't like people who are different from themselves. Who knows why? Maybe the difference scares them. Maybe they just don't understand it. We're all different though so there will always be differences among us. Our differences shouldn't matter. We should still show love and respect for each other, but you know it doesn't always work that way.

You can probably think of a story from your own life where there was an issue caused by a difference of thought, attitude or opinion. In this story, the difference was between Christians and those who were not. But God can turn any problem into a blessing, and that's what happened.

Every weekend my friend had a Bible study in his home. It was just a small study group. We weren't bothering anyone. One night we heard banging noises on the front of the house during our study. We looked out the window to see what the noise was and saw people throwing potatoes at our house. We couldn't figure out why, but later we learned they didn't like Christians.

They heard there was a Bible study going on at the house and decided to harass us by throwing potatoes. They thought we might take the study somewhere else if they did things to discourage us. They must not have known that God has a sense of humor.

You have to see the bigger picture in this story in order to understand the blessing. The family having the Bible study was unemployed. The husband had just lost his job. His wife was a stay-at-home mom, and they had children to provide for. They also had an extra mouth to feed since they were letting me live with them while I was unemployed too.

With no money coming in and several people living in the house, there wasn't a lot of food left in the pantry. We were getting hungry, so we asked God to send us something to eat.

He wanted to make something beautiful from the mess that had been my life up to this point.

God says, *"Trust in the Lord with all your heart..."* in Proverbs 3:5. He also says, *"But seek first the kingdom of God and His righteousness, and all these things shall be added to you."* (Matthew 6:33)

See, we had prayed for God to meet our needs, and He used that little bit of persecution for our good. We took those potatoes straight into our kitchen and cooked them all. There were so many potatoes we ate for a week or so. We had fried potatoes, mashed potatoes, potato pancakes and baked potatoes.

Praise God for meeting our need that day. He proved His Word can be trusted. There had been a lot of things happening in my life up to now and not everything was good. God was showing me how He was able to make something good out of a bad situation. He wanted to make something beautiful from the mess that had been my life up to this point. All that was needed was for me to trust and believe in His plan.

GOOD NEWS

"So, then faith comes by hearing, and
hearing by the word of God."
ROMANS 10:17

WHEN GOD COMES INTO YOUR LIFE and begins to change your heart, you want to reach out and save the whole world. The gospel was exciting to me. It changed my life, so everyone needed to know about it. I thought everyone would be as excited as me to hear about this good news.

With such drastic changes happening in my life, I thought my family would welcome the gospel with open arms. That was not how it happened though, and it shocked me. They said the gospel was good for me but to leave them alone about it.

Looking back on it now, they probably weren't sure if the change in my life was even true. Maybe they thought it was just some new phase that would pass. Eventually, they would see the change was real, but it would take some time.

So, my family wasn't willing to hear the message but there was still a burning inside of me to tell someone about Jesus. There was a group of people in Arkansas who were doing what was called street witnessing. That's where you go out into the streets and start talking randomly about the gospel with whoever comes across your path. This was my first day to go out with them.

There was an old man standing on a street corner by himself. We always started a street witnessing conversation by saying, *"Have you heard the Good News?"* It was kind of a catchy way to start a conversation about the gospel. Everyone wants to hear good news. That also happened to be what people were calling the gospel back in the '70's. When they said yes, we told them, *"Jesus is coming back soon!"*

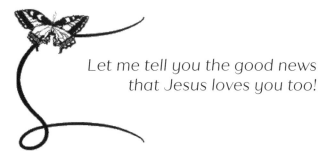

Let me tell you the good news that Jesus loves you too!

Well, that did not work well this time. The old man got mad at me. He said people had been telling him that since he was a little kid and he hadn't seen Jesus yet. He told me to go away and leave him alone. My family had already rejected me.

Can you imagine how the rejection felt as my first time out on the street? It was a horrible feeling that made me want to quit. I started back home with my head hanging low. There was a school on my way home, and a little boy started walking along the fence with me. He asked about the book underneath my arm. There was no answer, so he asked again.

I was too focused on my disappointment to really listen. He asked a third time and finally got my attention. Hey! He needs Jesus too! So, we talked how the Bible said Jesus loved him and died on a cross for him. The little boy asked God to forgive his sins and come live in his heart as his Savior that day.

It was my first time to pray with someone for salvation, and it felt so great. I love sharing the gospel and being used by God for His purposes. So, let me tell you the good news that Jesus loves you too!

HOW TO CATCH A SNORE

*"Now faith is the substance of things
hoped for, the evidence of things not seen."*
HEBREWS 11:1

THERE WERE SEVERAL people who let me live with them after my salvation. One of them was my pastor. He and his wife had a very big heart. They took me into their home and fed me. They got free TV dinners from a company the pastor worked for.

If the meal's weight wasn't correct, it couldn't be sold so they gave those meals to the preacher. We ate them almost every day. It was free food, so it was good food. The pastor ate the same thing for breakfast every day: two fried eggs, two pieces of toast and two strips of bacon with a cup of coffee. So much for cholesterol concerns. He's lived a long, happy life.

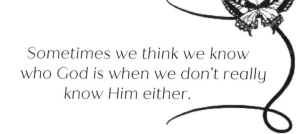

*Sometimes we think we know
who God is when we don't really
know Him either.*

While living with them, I worked at a gas station. There was a guy who hung around the station every night during my shift. He was living in boxes under the freeway bridge. When he told me where he was living, I invited him to come home with me.

Now, my home was actually a borrowed one, so it wasn't really my place to invite him inside. But surely the pastor would let him stay? They had an old car in their backyard, so he slept in the back seat of the car when he came home with me.

You could see the car from their kitchen window. The next morning as the pastor's wife was frying eggs for his breakfast, guess who she saw sleeping in the back seat of that old car? Yeah, you're right. My homeless friend.

She came into the bedroom her son shared with me and woke me up. She asked me who the guy in the car was. Now what would make her think this guy had anything to do with me?

Well, she told me to get up and pointed to the guy. We talked about him living in boxes and needing a place to sleep. So, she told me to bring him inside, and she fried him some eggs too.

Now, they have two homeless guys living with them. He was so dirty his long underwear could just about stand up on their own when he took them off, but she washed them for him.

Soon, he was rested, fed and smelled much better. The rest of us weren't getting much rest with him there though. This guy snored like a freight train. We tried to record him, but as soon as we got set up to hit the button, he woke up. Every time! We tried night after night but never got it done.

Years later, he admitted that he was actually a spy. Well, sort of. He was getting paid by my employer to hang around the gas station and make sure I wasn't stealing from him.

So, you might not really know the person you think you know. Sometimes we think we know who God is when we don't really know Him either. If you think you know who God is based on what someone else has told you about Him, why don't you try finding out who He is and what He's like for yourself?

The Bible is where you'll find Him. Prayer is a great way to begin your search.

JESUS MINISTRY

*"I thank my God upon every remembrance
of you, always in every prayer of mine
making request for you all with joy, for
your fellowship in the gospel from the first
day until now, being confident of this very
thing, that He who has begun a good work
in you will complete it until the day
of Jesus Christ."*
PHILIPPIANS 1:3-6

A JESUS MINISTRY IN LITTLE ROCK was home to me for a little while. They did lots of street witnessing all over Arkansas. Everyone there lived in two big houses. One house for the guys and another for the girls. There was a big room in between that was used for meetings. They raised money to support the house and their ministry events by selling paintings.

Everyone who lived there took turns going on the road for a week or two to sell the paintings. They bought the paintings cheap in Mexico and then sold them for more. Sometimes we traveled to attend concerts. My job was to hand out what they called *Jesus Free Papers*. The papers advertised the concert and shared testimonies of the people in our group.

And, of course, they talked about God. I really like to talk about God, so this job was perfect for me.

Mountainview, Arkansas, was one of my favorite places to go. It was a beautiful little town. While walking around the courthouse there to minister one day, this guy came running over yelling, *"Didn't I whip one of you boys the last time you were here?"*

My fighting days were supposed to be in the past. Unsure what to think and not knowing what to do either, I just started praying and telling God this guy was about to pounce all over me, like He didn't know it already. What did He want me to do? Were we supposed to fight or what? It was sure looking like we might.

Now, the Word of God says our ways are not His ways (Isaiah 55:8) and that is so true. God answered me with a question: *"What are you doing here?"*

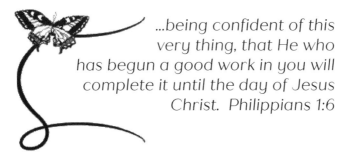

...being confident of this very thing, that He who has begun a good work in you will complete it until the day of Jesus Christ. Philippians 1:6

Handing out free papers was my job, so maybe he should get one. That logic didn't make much sense to me but, just as the guy was unbuttoning his shirt for a fight, he got a little piece of paper anyway and something sounding pretty wimpy came out of my mouth: *"I don't know if you whipped one of us before or not but here is a free paper."*

He grabbed it while asking if it was about drugs. With his shirt already halfway removed, he heard me say boldly this time: *"No, sir. As a matter of fact, it's about Jesus."*

He stopped right there and buttoned up his shirt. He started telling me about his heart problems and all kinds of other things. We talked for a while and he was invited to our concert down the road that night. He said he would come but he didn't. God knew what He was doing though. It taught me to listen for God's leading more often.

One day while sitting on the edge of the stage during a break in the festival, two people came over to talk with me. They were sitting in seats at the front of the stage listening to me share my testimony. We talked together like we were the only people there.

When we finished talking, we saw the rest of the chairs were now full of people. It scared me to realize they had all been listening to me talk from the stage. It was the first time my testimony was shared with a large crowd other than a church group, and it was a blessing to me.

After that, we heard about a rock group coming to Little Rock. We loved events where we could pass out tracts about Jesus. We loved any chance to be able to witness and pray with people.

So, we went to this concert ready to share. A cool thing happened there during intermission. One of our guys got into the building when they were in between performances.

Now you have to know this guy. He acted a little crazy, but he was cool. He had long hair and always walked around with his hands behind his back. For some reason, his head wobbled so he looked stoned all the time, but he was just high on Jesus.

My friend went inside, walked to the stage and, looking stoned with his head all wobbly, asked the guy on the stage if he could come up and say something cool to everybody. The guy actually let him.

My friend walked onto the stage, picked up the microphone and asked everyone if they wanted to hear some good news. They yelled, *"Yeah!"* Then he told them Jesus loved them, and the whole building got silent.

He told them Jesus died for all the wrongs they had ever done and provided forgiveness if they would only ask Him. No one stopped him. He said thanks when he was done and left the stage.

It was amazing. Several people prayed with us to ask Jesus to forgive them of their sins that night on the steps after the concert.

The times of ministry with this group were really special for me. They were just the beginning of a lifetime of ministry. That's God's desire for you and me.

You don't have to be a TV evangelist to be used by God. He uses us right where we are and equips us with everything we need for life and godliness in this world. (2 Peter 1:3) There's no greater fulfillment in life than to serve the Lord and watch His transforming power at work within the lives around you.

PIZZA OR CHICKEN

"Be anxious for nothing, but in everything
by prayer and supplication,
with thanksgiving, let your requests be
made known to God."
PHILIPPIANS 4:6

ONE OF MY FRIENDS managed a pizza restaurant in Arkansas. The business was having money issues. He hired me, but God put it on my heart to help him out by working for free. My friend agreed to give me a spot in the back room to sleep in exchange for pay. He also let me eat free.

There was plenty of pizza, chicken and salad. He didn't have the beer taps open because he was a Christian. We had a blast there praying for people and having Bible studies. You would have thought it was a church instead of a pizza place.

One evening two guys came in for pizza. The older guy was a preacher. His nephew was the star performer in a musical, and they were in town for his play. They were surprised to see that we prayed for the people who came in to eat. We told them we would pray with anyone who wanted prayer. We didn't pray with everyone, but we did pray for everyone.

We let them know we would gladly pray for them if they wanted. The nephew said he was a piano player and his hands were having trouble playing. He said he didn't really believe in healing, but we did! We said it would be interesting to see what God had in His plan for him, so we prayed.

After prayer, he asked if we thought he was healed. We answered by asking what he thought. That was way more important than what we thought.

This pizza restaurant just happened to have a piano. He started playing and then stopped in the middle of the song. He was stopped for a while and then started playing again. This time he played the song all the way through with big tears on his cheeks.

He played several songs, and even his uncle had tears by the time he finished playing. The uncle asked if we thought God could heal his eyesight. Why couldn't He? We prayed for him and then stepped outside. He said he could see the apartment buildings in the distance and read the writing on the side of a school bus parked there.

He ran back inside to tell his nephew and they both cried again. They were not having pizza that night. They were having church. Stories like this happened all the time there.

God is good all the time.

The restaurant was doing better, and my friend was finally able to hire more employees. He tried to pay me now, but I still wouldn't let him. Working there was getting old though, so I was praying for a way out. It wasn't happening, and my discouragement was growing.

Did you know God's Word says there's a way of escape for every temptation we face? (1 Cor. 10:13) We still have to be willing to watch for His way though. One night, the only people in the building were the assistant manager and me.

He was in the office doing paperwork when he saw me turn on the beer tap and pour myself a pitcher. He asked what was going on and told me to come sit in his office. We talked about my discouragement and being fed up because God wasn't meeting my need. We talked about needing a home, but there was no place for me to go. Staying there was driving me nuts. If God wasn't going to provide, then why not give up and get drunk?

At that very moment, the phone rang. It was a friend of mine. She said she had heard about me needing a place to stay, but I was too upset to listen. I hung up the phone, leaned back in my chair and chugged that pitcher of beer.

The phone rang, and it was her again. I was already knocked out. I hadn't drank in so long, that pitcher of beer flat knocked me on my tail. I woke in a little room with all my stuff on a dresser. That was weird because there was no remembrance of how my things got there.

The mobile home was unfamiliar to me. My good friend was standing in the hallway. At that moment, it became clear what had happened. She didn't speak with me when she called the second time, but the assistant manager talked with her.

It was so foolish of me. God provided but, in my discouragement, His way of escape was ignored. Giving up and getting drunk wasn't the answer. God heard me, but I gave up hope too soon. That mobile home was provided rent free for a while and someone even gave me another job. Yes, God is good all the time, even when we're low on faith.

TWO MINUTE PRAYER

"But, beloved, do not forget this one thing,
that with the Lord one day is as a thousand
years, and a thousand years as one day.
The Lord is not slack concerning His
promise, as some count slackness, but is
longsuffering toward us, not willing that
any should perish but that all
should come to repentance."
II PETER 3:8-9

TWO OF MY FRIENDS had nowhere to live, so I moved out of the place where I was staying with friends and told these two guys they could live in my car with me. We were all young, single and trying to figure our lives out. My car had two flat tires, but it was home for us now. We took turns trading out sleeping arrangements in the car.

One night two of us would sleep scrunched up in the front seat and the other one would stretch out in the back. We traded places the next night so every third night you could sleep pretty well. We parked the car in an apartment complex parking lot where another friend lived. He let us use his bathroom and shower.

We had Bible studies at the friend's apartment that were a blessing, but it seemed like something was missing. It wasn't something you could put your finger on. Then one night it occurred to me that we were getting into gospel music more than prayer. That was what was missing. So, one night while everyone else went out for something to eat, I stayed home and kneeled beside the bed to pray for two things.

First, one of my brothers in the Lord had given up on God. He had gotten so wrapped up with motocross racing that he had left God out of his life. So, my prayer was that he would remember God.

Next, I prayed my friends would get back into prayer like we used to do. When my prayers were finished, it felt like God was breathing on me and He said my prayers were answered. About that time, there was a tap on my shoulder.

It was my friend who had gotten involved with motocross. He wanted to check on me because I had been in there a long time, and he was worried. It didn't feel like it was a long time. They were just two little prayers.

That made me think about how God's Word says, "With the Lord one day is as a thousand years and a thousand years as one day." He said he would give me another minute, but he didn't leave. Instead, he stood there. He said he couldn't leave because there was an angel in the doorway who wanted him to give his life back to Jesus.

WOW! That blew my mind! So, we prayed together on our knees. It touched us both so much we looked like two crybabies. We were still on our knees crawling to the bathroom to blow our noses when the bedroom door next to us opened. One of our friends asked if we wanted to join their prayer meeting. Yes, we did!

God had answered both of my prayers right then and thinking about it just blew me away. God's Word says that if we pray and believe, He will answer our prayers.

Just think about it: "Ask, and it will be given to you; seek and you will find; knock and it will be opened to you." (Matthew 7:7)

No one will be homeless in Heaven.

There are so many other promises God has given us in His Word. If something's missing in your life, just have a talk with Him. He loves to hear from you, and He has the answer.

One of the best promises Jesus gives is the one that says He's coming back to take us home to be with Him someday. No one will be homeless in heaven because He has gone there to prepare a place in His Father's house for all those who love Him. (John 14:2-3)

That's a family reunion to look forward to!

BROTHER OR FRIEND?

"But above all these things put on love,
which is the bond of perfection."
COLOSSIANS 3:14

TWO FRIENDS who were brothers in the Lord were letting me stay at their apartment with them. One of them didn't get along well with me. We fought about everything. We slept in separate rooms. We separated our food. We even did our nightly Bible study from separate rooms with the doors open so we wouldn't have to see each other.

One night as we were studying, we read John 15:13. It said, *"Greater love has no one than this, than to lay down one's life for his friends."* They kept on reading, but my eyes stopped on that verse.

My thoughts were on our friendship, which wasn't a good one. God wanted to teach us all something from that verse. It felt like God wanted me to get off the couch and go talk with my brothers in Christ about that verse. It wasn't something I wanted to do but knew I had to.

When he saw me standing there, the guy who didn't like me asked, "What are you doing in my room?" I told him God wanted me to share something with him. He said to say it fast and get out.

I explained God had shown me that sometimes when we have friends over to stay the night, our brother might pick on the friend and we would defend our friend against our brother. That's because brothers fight.

God had shown me that was our problem. We were treating each other like brothers and had forgotten we needed to be friends too. We had trouble loving each other for that reason. We weren't friends. If we stopped thinking of each other as brothers and started treating each other as friends, we could love each other with greater love.

We were treating each other like brothers and had forgotten we needed to be friends too.

God asked me to ask my Christian brother to be my friend that day. It was hard, but it melted our hearts. He started to cry and said he wanted to be my friend. Then we both cried. We never fought again after that.

GOD SAID JUMP

"Let your conduct be without covetousness;
be content with such things as you have.
For He Himself has said, I will never leave
you nor forsake you."
HEBREWS 13:5

WHEN YOU FIRST GET SAVED, people call you a baby Christian. I hated that. I was eighteen years old and definitely not a baby. Babies had to be taught and depended on other people to take care of them.

Most kids my age were just beginning to leave home but not me. I had been taking care of myself for a long time. There was no need for anyone to take care of me.

There was a lot to be learned about God and how to live the life God wanted me to live though. Except for going to church with my aunt a few times as a kid and during basic training in the Army, my ears hadn't heard much about God at all.

Even though being called a baby rubbed me the wrong way, it was true when it came to being a Christian. Depending on others was something new to me, and it was a really big step. My heart had been shut tight to other people for a long time. Life had taught me that opening your heart would get you hurt and depending on anyone but yourself would leave you empty-handed. People weren't trustworthy.

Christians preached a lot about loving one another. They weren't like the other people who had been in my life. This was the first time in a long time my heart had been open to anyone. They taught me to love and trust them, so it really hurt to learn they could disappoint me too. The people who had been there as spiritual leaders for me wouldn't always be. God wants us to learn to walk on our own by faith and trust in Him. That was happening today, and it was not an easy lesson.

On this day, a friend told me he was giving up on God. That floored me. I went to tell another friend about that guy, and he said he was too! What was this world coming to? These were the guys that led me to the Lord and now they wanted to quit?

Confused and feeling really down, I thought about another friend who could pray with me and went to his house to tell him about these two guys. That's when he said he was giving up too. This could not be happening.

The thought came to me to give up too. I folded a suicide note and left it with my friend before taking off, just walking around with no idea of where to go. Going back to my old life was not an option.

If my new life wasn't going to be any better than the old one, then it would be best to end it all now. Their news was so upsetting that nothing mattered anymore. While walking across the Arkansas River Bridge toward Little Rock, it occurred to me that jumping off the bridge into the river would be a good way to end it.

So, I climbed over the rail, put my heels on the edge, held on with my hands and leaned way out over the river. Then God said to jump. You might have expected Him to say not to, but it went just the other way. God said, "*JUMP!*"

Now that surprised me. It interrupted the little pity party going on inside my head. It seemed like God ought to have a little sympathy for me. Instead, He said to end it.

So, my hands let go of the rails and my body started falling forward toward the river, but the water wasn't there. When my eyes opened to look for it, my hands were still holding on to the bridge. Then God spoke to my heart.

He said, *"Now that the old man has jumped, are you ready to start living your new life for me?"* I jumped to the other side of the rail and ran down the road praising God.

My pastor pulled up in his car and rolled the window down to offer me a ride. He had heard about the note and was out searching for me. That was my pastor for you. He took me to a friend's house. Everyone was there.

They had all been out looking for me. Someone told them about my note and spread the word. The ones that had given up on God were there, and they had changed their minds. We were one big happy family again. When they heard what happened on the bridge, they were all praising God with me.

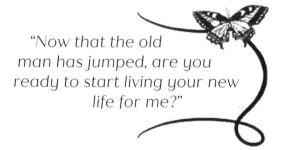

"Now that the old man has jumped, are you ready to start living your new life for me?"

See, what God made me realize on that bridge is that we need to serve HIM. Not our friend's God, but our God. We must depend on God. We cannot depend on men. There are a lot of problems with that.

Men will fail you because they aren't perfect, even if they're Christians. They can't be everything we think they should be because they're not perfect. God alone is perfect.

HE is everything we need. HE should be everything we want. HE is sufficient for us. This was an important lesson for me, and this was the day my faith really began to grow. This is an important lesson for you, too.

Know this: God wants to be the One you count on above all others. He can and will provide for you if you just ask and believe. Allow Him to work in your life, and He will. That's grown-up Christianity, folks.

LOVE YOU LIKE CRAZY

"He who finds a wife finds a good thing
and obtains favor from the LORD."
PROVERBS 18:22

WHEN WE FIRST GOT MARRIED, I did some crazy things and embarrassed my wife a lot. Who knows why she married me? She saw something in me that others didn't see, including myself. God must have helped her see past all the rude and crude things about me. She loved me somehow in spite of all my faults, and I've loved her with my whole heart from the very first moment my eyes saw her.

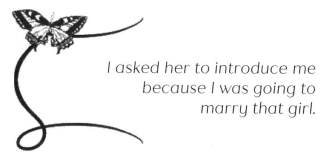

I asked her to introduce me because I was going to marry that girl.

I was asleep in our car while waiting for a little Christian youth ministry to begin one night in North Little Rock, Arkansas, when some car doors woke me. There she was getting out of her car. The license plate on the car said Texas, so I went in and asked the lady who ran the ministry if she knew the girl from Texas. She said they were family and wanted to know why. I asked her to introduce me because I was going to marry that girl. She said I was crazy.

We had only known each other two weeks when I asked her dad for permission to marry her. Oh, wait. Let me explain that more correctly. Actually, I didn't ask her dad. I asked her to ask her mom to ask her dad for his permission.

That's a great way to make a good impression on your future in-laws. My fear was that he would say no and that he might kill me. She was a nice girl and, well, I wasn't exactly a nice guy.

My mother-in-law, who became Mom to me, replied with what would be the first of many lessons learned from my new family. She wouldn't ask him. She said that was my responsibility. Really? Now that was a new word for me. When I did ask her dad, to my amazement, he agreed.

When I asked her to marry me the first time, we had only met a week earlier. She thought it was a joke, but it wasn't. So, the question was repeated the next week, a little more seriously, and she said yes! That was the end of October 1976.

We were married by mid-December. We had known each other only two months when we married. She was in her senior year of high school. Almost every day during her senior year, I took a single rose to her at school.

They wouldn't let me take it to her in class, so it was left in the dean's office for her to pick up at the end of the day. The office staff got so excited seeing me bring that rose for her.

When we got married, my wife had everything. The car, the furniture and the little chest filled with all the stuff she had been collecting for when she would have a home of her own.

There wasn't any advance planning on my part, so my contribution was only a pillowcase full of belongings. Her dad found a garage apartment for us to rent nearby. He had me go with him to talk to the landlord about making arrangements to pay out our first month's rent and deposit.

Her dad had actually talked with the older couple before and given them a check to hold in case we didn't come thru. We didn't know about that until much later. I'm so grateful for this man's influence on my life and am glad they never had to cash his check. Her father was one of the best men I've ever known. I wasn't used to having someone believe in me and never wanted to let her or her parents down.

It was time to get serious about getting a job and go to work for a living. Remember, the streets were my home for much of my life so there wasn't any rent or utilities to pay. Employer expectations weren't something learned on the street. There was a need to change some old ways as a Christian and still a lot to learn about responsibility.

My wife's brother and I stayed out playing in the snow almost all night one night. We had a blast. There were a lot of hills where we lived, and we went sliding up and down as many as we could that night. When my wife woke me for work the next morning, my plan was to sleep in.

That plan didn't go over well with her. Needless to say, there was no skipping work that day. No one told me growing up would be so hard.

My wife had a car when we got married. I did not so I walked to work. My job wasn't far from our house, and my feet had taken me everywhere before we got married so they were used to walking. My mother-in-law offered to give me a ride. She would come to pick me up some days, but I felt bad taking rides from her. I would find somewhere to hide, and she would circle the block looking for me.

She finally got tired of that and told me not to ask for a ride. She was just kidding. At least, that's what I hoped because when it was snowing, a ride would be nice. My mother-in-law is the best there is, and she is a blessing to me.

One day we went into a fabric store. I thought it would be fun to embarrass my wife and her mom while they were at the checkout. I stood near the entrance and started reaching up into the air grabbing something imaginary to put into my mouth. I looked pretty silly.

When they left the store, I followed them all the way to the car while continuing to grab something from the air. There was no reason to do this other than craziness. When we got into the car, they were not embarrassed at all.

Instead, they were laughing. So why were they laughing? They said the lady in line in front of them nodded her head my way and told the cashier there was a man behaving strangely at the front door. The cashier smiled and told the lady it would be okay because that man came in there all the time acting crazy. The joke was on me that day.

On another day while walking through the mall with my wife, everyone was smiling at us. My wife wondered why everyone was looking at us. What she didn't know about was my pair of glasses with these eyeballs hanging down.

The eyeballs bounced around as we walked, but my face was turned away from her so she couldn't see them.

I turned toward her and said, *"I don't know why everyone is looking at us. Do you?"*

On another day, my wife and her cousin went to the mall to shop. Her cousin's husband was a big guy with a long beard wearing overalls. He was a hat collector and bought a black top hat while we were there. I bought a bright red umbrella hat.

So here we are walking through the mall together. This guy wearing farmer overalls and a top hat, and me in a business suit and tie with an umbrella sitting on my head. We thought we looked pretty cool and couldn't understand why our wives wouldn't walk with us.

How did my wife put up with my craziness? I don't know, but we've had fun. Crazy and fun was a lot different from the hateful, unhappy guy I had been before. There was a lot of learning and growing yet to do, but my life had changed so much already.

It was full of joy now. There was a reason to live, a smile on my face and something to look forward to each day. Something to live for is what God gives you.

Ernie and Julie—ABOVE in 1976
just before they were married
and BELOW in 2018

OUR CHRISTIAN WOODSTOCK

*"Therefore, by Him let us continually offer
the sacrifice of praise to God, that is,
the fruit of our lips, giving thanks to His
name. But do not forget to do good
and to share, for with such sacrifices God
is well pleased."*
HEBREWS 13:15-16

IT WAS SOMETIME in the late 1970's when a bunch of us decided to have what we called our Christian Woodstock in Arkansas. It was one of the best times of my life. A friend of mine ran a Christian bookstore, and he was able to use his contacts to get it put together.

We found a place in the Ozark Mountains and asked the people that owned the land if we could have it there. It was the perfect place. There were hills all around and a large open space with no homes on the property. We scheduled the recording artists and then couldn't decide how to get them from the airport to our location in the mountains. You know God always meets your need.

The owner of the courier service that employed me at the time leased his cars and trucks from a local Ford dealership. He knew the owner well and asked if he could help us out. Man, did he ever! He let us have a new Ford Bronco four-wheel drive truck and a large covered trailer for only a few dollars a day with no mileage charges.

This was perfect. My boss gave me the week off. My assignment was to pick up the musicians from the airport and drive them to the concert area in the Ozarks. Those who had already performed had to be returned back to the airport in Little Rock for their departure flight. Every day there were different musicians to pick up and return. It was a lot of driving but so much fun.

We had so many gospel groups there. It was a true blessing to meet all those musicians. We had a great time of fellowship plus they gave me free albums! People paid admission to the event, and we paid the bands as they performed.

There were people spread all over the mountainside with tents and stuff. It looked just like Woodstock, just not quite as many people and with contemporary gospel music instead. We used two flatbed trailers sitting end-to-end as the stage and powered it all with big generators. It was a wonderful time of worship.

The hardest part of coordinating it was dealing with production managers. You didn't deal with the band directly until they got there. Everything was handled through their manager.

The last artist who performed was well known but he'll need to remain nameless for this story. He was the last artist picked up from the airport, and we had run out of money to finish paying him. We had already paid his retainer and travel costs but didn't have the remaining fee he required.

It was my responsibility to give him the news that we couldn't pay him when he got off the plane. We talked about it, and he was given an apology with an option to catch the next flight back to Nashville without performing. He told me that he didn't care what his manager would say. He said he came to worship God with us and that's what he intended to do.

What a guy! He was one of my favorite artists before this, and now he was even more so. I offered to take him back to our house for dinner before the long ride to the Ozarks. He took me up on it, so we went to my in-laws' home and ate fried chicken.

Then we left for the mountains. He did what God sent him to do and flew back home. Apparently, we failed to plan properly for this event, but this man's attitude has been remembered with respect for a long time.

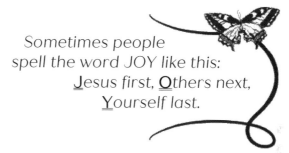

Sometimes people
spell the word JOY like this:
Jesus first, Others next,
Yourself last.

Sometimes people spell the word JOY like this: Jesus first, Others next, Yourself last. His response to what happened is a perfect picture of the joy that comes from serving others.

We couldn't pay his fee then, but we received enough money from people with outstanding obligations after the event that we were able to bless this artist with more than the fee he was contracted for.

That's how God works sometimes. We received blessing upon blessing that week, and souls were saved all during the concert. God bless this brother for being willing to serve like he did, and praise God for His gifts to us also.

MACHINE SHOP MIRACLE

*"No temptation has overtaken you except
such as is common to man; but God is
faithful, who will not allow you to be
tempted beyond what you are able, but
with the temptation will also make the way
of escape, that you may be able to bear it."*
I CORINTHIANS 10:13

SITTING IN THE BALCONY of the church on Sunday morning is probably not the best time or place to be thinking about how to kill someone, but that's what was happening on this day. Let me tell you about what happened to get me to that place in my life.

My wife's uncle had gotten me a job at a machine shop that made parts for the oilfield: liners, pumps, pistons, etc. My job was running a face and bevel machine. It was a good job, but the shop was really dirty. Some of the guys that worked there became good buddies with me, but there was one guy who didn't like me very much.

He pretty much hated me, and no one could figure out why. He hit me and threw machine parts at me to try to hurt me almost every day. He wrapped a wire around my neck trying to strangle me one day, and he put a gun to my head once. Hopefully, he wouldn't have pulled the trigger, but he sure made my life awful for about a year.

It was hard to sit back and take it. I really wanted to let him have it, but since becoming a Christian about three years earlier there had been a lot of talk about turning the other cheek. So now there was a lot of prayer about how to show the love of Jesus to this guy without striking back. It was tough to have self-control, but the other guys in the shop were watching to see what my response would be. They had been listening to me tell them about the love of Jesus, so this was not the time to fail.

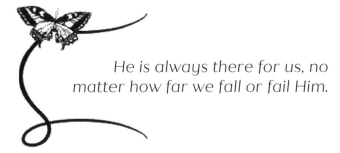

He is always there for us, no matter how far we fall or fail Him.

The guys in the shop didn't like the way he was treating me either. Some days they took him out back and threatened to whip him if he didn't leave me alone. He would back off for a few days, but then he went right back to the way he was before.

God's Word says we shouldn't fight or hate another person, but how long are you really supposed to turn the other cheek? It was getting harder and harder to love this guy like God wanted me to, and all of us wondered how long it would be before there was a breaking point. This was it.

In the balcony of the church that Sunday, the decision was made. God wasn't answering my prayers, so He must not care. This guy wasn't going to stop harassing me on his own, and God wasn't going to stop him.

In my mind, the only way he would stop was if he was dead, so the question became how to do it. My idea was to take my knife to work, slit his throat and then bang his face on the floor until no one could recognize him.

After church that day, I sharpened my knife and told my wife about the plan that might put me in prison. She said, *"Just trust God. He will provide for you."* She wasn't worried. Instead, she prayed. It's a good thing she was strong in faith that day because mine was weak.

The next morning my knife went with me to work. Every morning before our shift began, the guys all sat around drinking coffee on three benches that were placed together in a U shape. While we were sitting there that morning, they listened to me tell them about my plan to stop this guy from treating me the way he did.

If he came in and started any trouble, his Adam's apple was going to be pulled from the slit in his throat and fed to him as he died. They all thought it was a joke until they saw the knife. Then they were told that I would look them up for revenge after release from prison if they didn't back me up by saying it was self-defense. They looked at me like my mind had been lost. It had.

The guy came into the shop, and everyone scooted away from me. My hand was already holding the knife handle ready to strike. The guy walked right up to me, looked me straight in the eye and said, *"I've got something to say to you."*

My grip became even tighter on the knife, and my eyes were focused on his throat right below his ear thinking about how to slit him open from that ear to the other one. What he said next shocked us all. He said he had been thinking and realized the only reason he picked on me was because he saw Jesus in my life, and he didn't have that.

WHAT!?!? He didn't have Jesus in his life? That was the reason? Now what?

The guys sitting on the benches had their jaws open and their tongues hanging out like cartoon characters. They were stunned. When he heard me say what was planned for him that day, he was stunned too. The knife was still in my pocket. His face turned white as a ghost when he saw it.

We talked a lot that morning. During the lunch break, we went back behind the liners where the guys used to take him to tell him to leave me alone. We got on our knees, and he gave his life to the Lord that day.

It made me think of something Corrie Ten Boom said regarding the time she spent in a Holocaust concentration camp. Her family helped hide Jews during the war and were eventually sent to the camps as punishment. She and her family endured horrible things during that time. Her father and sister died in the camps.

She knew how it felt to suffer, and she also understood forgiveness. She shared how her sister had encouraged her to guard her heart against bitterness and to trust God's plan even thru pain. She quoted her sister as saying, *"No pit is so deep that He is not deeper still."*

What a true statement. He is always there for us, no matter how far we fall or fail Him. Sometimes we forget this in our darkest moments. I had forgotten this on that day, but He had not forgotten me.

GOD LOVES BIKERS

*"For I am not ashamed of the gospel of
Christ, for it is the power of God to
salvation for everyone who believes..."*
ROMANS 1:16

WE LIVED IN Arkansas when we were first married. My wife was from Texas, and we decided to move back there after a while because the job opportunities were better. So, Houston here we come! It was also exciting to be moving because we would be living closer to the rest of her family again.

Her mom had a cousin there that the family wanted me to get to know. He was living a rough life as biker, which is why everyone thought I should talk with him. Since my past included some friendships with bikers and was pretty wild before giving my life to the Lord, they thought he might listen to me. So, they tried to get us connected after our move.

Her cousin was also an ex-convict. He had gotten out of prison not long before we moved to Houston. His gut had been filled with bullets by two bikers who didn't like him. They left him to die by a dumpster behind a store in the woods. Someone found him there and took him to the hospital to get fixed up.

So, he had lived and now the family wanted me to talk to him about the Lord. He had spent his whole life in and out of prison. They thought he was mean and evil. But he had a wife and kids, so they wanted to see a change take place in his heart. The family introduced me to him after our move to Houston.

They were right. This guy wasn't a biker from one of those recreational Harley groups that take off for pleasure rides on the weekend. He had the rough biker look: dirty jeans, cuts, boots, hip knife, bad smell and bad language. Riding was his way of life. He thought he was so tough he couldn't change. He didn't know all things are possible with God. (Mark 10:27)

My wife also had an uncle who thought he was tough. He wasn't a real biker. He was a "wanna-be" biker who hung out with this cousin trying to be like him. My wife asked me to give him and his girlfriend a ride to the doctor one day. He was mad, cussing up a storm and pulled a gun out in the car threatening his girlfriend like a crazy man. Oh, that wasn't going to happen!

So, the car came to a stop. He was told to put that thing away or he would have to deal with me crawling into the backseat to take it away from him. Now who was acting crazy? He could have shot me in the head and ended that conversation, but he looked at me and put it away instead. Guess he figured he should listen to anyone crazy enough to say that to him while holding a gun in his hand. Years later, that uncle gave me the privilege of leading him to the Lord. Praise God!

He didn't know all things are possible with God.

So, about the cousin. He was a true tough guy. The kind that made a lot of people feel uncomfortable. But he liked me and accepted my friendship. God just took control and used me as His messenger. He still challenged me every now and then to see if he could scare me, but he always lost.

Eventually, he gave his life to the Lord. He used to joke that the Bible talked about motorcycles because Exodus 15:1 says, *"Then Moses and the children of Israel sang this song to the Lord, and spoke, saying, I will sing to the LORD, for He has <u>triumphed</u> gloriously! The horse and its rider He has thrown into the sea!"* He would say Moses rode a Triumph, laughing out loud. It was a corny joke, but it was funny hearing the "tough guy" tell it.

We spent many nights on our knees by the sofa praying and reading scripture. He still had issues to work through, but he sincerely loved the Lord. Most of his family didn't believe that was true. He told so many lies over the years that it was hard for them to trust him. He understood. He said it was okay because God knew his heart and that was what mattered most.

He was shot and killed by another biker later so right now he's a biker in heaven. Having the chance to pray and lead these two men to the Lord was a privilege. We'll get to see each other again when we all get to heaven someday. Praise God that there really are happily ever after endings.

FAITH AT WORK

"And whatever you do, do it heartily, as to
the Lord and not to men."
COLOSSIANS 3:23

BACK IN THE 1980'S, my wife was pregnant with our second child. The oil industry took a hit, and it cost a lot of us our jobs. That included me. The machine shop that hired me decided to lay a bunch of us off, and it left me wondering what to do now?

All the labor office had to offer was a bunch of people standing in line looking for work. We prayed and decided if we couldn't find work, then work would have to be created. We had kids to feed, right?

We knew someone who had recently started his own business painting addresses on curbs in front of people's houses. So, with his idea in mind, we went to the store and got some curb-marking paint, some two-inch paint rollers and masking tape. We bought a set of brass number stencils that hooked together. Then we bought a little tray that had four pockets with a handle and some chalk. We were ready for business.

Well, almost. We needed a method and a sales pitch. We decided it would be best to work as a team, so we found someone else who needed a job to pair up with.

We selected a neighborhood to target for the day and walked from house to house down each street looking for sales. Making the sales pitch was my job. My partner followed behind to complete the job.

After knocking on the front door, each customer who answered heard a sales pitch that sounded something like this: "*Hello. We're in your neighborhood today placing nighttime security identification numbers on curbs for families using white florescent paint. The kind they use to paint stripes on the roads with.*"

At that time, the sales pitch hesitated to wait for a nod showing they understood. Then we would say: "*We use this to paint your house number on your curb so that if you ever need the police or an ambulance in an emergency, they can find your address quickly. We use a wire brush to clean the curb where you would like the number placed, tape it off and spray the number on the curb using special stencils.*

When we're done, you can come out to inspect, and we'll collect payment upon your satisfaction with the job. All we need to know is where you want it. Would you prefer to have it placed on the curb for six bucks or on the inside of your driveway also, like most of your neighbors, so traffic coming either direction can see it really well for ten?"

Then it was time to stop talking and wait for a reply. Most of the time they bought it. If they did, their curb was marked with chalk for my partner who was following along behind me to clean and paint. We collected money afterward if they liked it. They weren't charged anything if they didn't.

Sometimes we painted an entire neighborhood. Every single curb. It was amazing how much cash came in doing this.

We also formed a little wholesale business with one of my buddies where we sold fold-up sunglasses in a carry case. We sold them by the pair or the box. Each box held a dozen pair. We made money either way, and it helped keep the bills paid.

Between painting curbs and selling sunglasses, we paid a lot of bills during those months of unemployment. Times were hard without jobs back then, but at the end of every day there was money. Praise the Lord, God always provided for us.

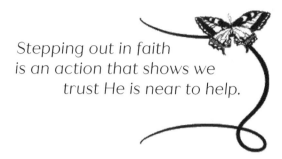

Stepping out in faith is an action that shows we trust He is near to help.

You really shouldn't have to go without work. Sometimes you may have to get creative about ways to bring in an income, and it may take more than one job to make ends meet. We like to blame God for things that go wrong in our life, but we don't always want to do anything to help ourselves.

While the Bible doesn't exactly say *"God helps those who help themselves,"* it does say, *"If anyone will not work, neither shall he eat."* (2 Thessalonians 3:10) God wants to provide, but He doesn't want us to be lazy either. He wants us to ask Him for our needs and trust Him to take care of us. He also wants us to be willing to step out in faith.

Stepping out in faith is an action that shows we trust He is near to help. My faith wasn't huge at the time, but it only takes a little. Just one little baby step really, and you'll find He'll meet you there.

MICHAEL JACKSON REPLAY

*"That the genuineness of your faith, being
much more precious than gold that
perishes, though it is tested by fire, may be
found to praise, honor, and glory at the
revelation of Jesus Christ..."*
1 PETER 1:7

WE WERE IN THE COUNTRY visiting my wife's aunt and uncle. We were out squirrel hunting when her uncle decided to cut down a small tree. He got an axe, and we began chopping. In the middle of our chopping, we realized the dirt hill we were standing on was actually an ant hill.

Ants were already all over us. Our pants came off and then our underwear as we tried to get the ants off our bodies. It's a good thing we were in a field far away from everyone because it was pretty embarrassing dancing around naked trying to get those ants out of our pants.

On Sunday, we all went to church. The field next to their house was on fire when we got home. Her uncle called the fire department. It was a volunteer unit, and they came running. They all had brooms trying to brush the fire inward so it wouldn't spread further.

This was a small town with an old yellow firetruck that you had to push to start. It didn't hold much water either, and they had to go to the pond with a suction hose to fill it up. The truck had died. They couldn't get it started again, and it was sitting right by the grass that was on fire.

Folks, this was a huge grass fire, and the truck was about to be engulfed by flames. We all had to stop fighting the fire to push-start the truck. Have you ever tried to push-start a firetruck full of water in the middle of a field while it's in flames? It's not easy.

It can be risky putting yourself out there for others.

We finally got it started and went back to brushing the fire inward with our little brooms. The guy with the hose from the truck was standing next to me. Some of the guys were brushing the fire side-to-side instead of inward, which causes fireballs to fly up into the air. We knew that could start a fire behind us, so we were telling one of the guys how he was causing these fireballs to go flying everywhere when, all of a sudden, one flew up and landed on top of my head. My hair was on fire!

Good thing the guy with the firehose was standing right next to me. He sprayed the top of my head to put out the fire. That was good, but it burned the hair right down the middle of my head. My hair was long, and the top center of my head was burned so now there was a big bald spot with a blister right in the top middle of my head.

People called it the Michael Jackson replay because it happened the same week his hair caught fire while filming a Pepsi commercial. Everyone called me Michael all weekend, but at least her uncle's field wasn't on fire anymore.

This story is funny now, but it wasn't at the time. Just think how differently the story might have ended if we hadn't all been there to help. Even though it caused some pain, it was good we were there to help our family.

That's how it should be with our Christian family too. It can be risky putting yourself out there for others. Sometimes we're afraid of getting bit or burnt, and that might happen to you. God says we can expect to have persecution (2 Timothy 3:12) and tribulation (John 16:33) in this life. We shouldn't let that stop us from being there though. The end is worth the effort, especially if it's for the sake of the gospel. And remember, God has overcome the world

COPS ON THE BALL

"I will sing of mercy and justice; To You,
O LORD, I will sing praises."
PSALM 101:1

MY JOB WORKING for a delivery service used to have me driving all over the Houston area. A car with an older couple in it stopped beside me at a stoplight one day. While we were sitting there, a car came speeding toward us in my rearview mirror.

It slammed into the car with the older couple and sent them flying through the red light. The car that hit them landed in a ditch. My company van was not hit.

As I got out to check on the older couple, four guys got out of the car that was in the ditch and took off down the road. The older couple was shook up a little, but they were okay.

A little red truck pulled up to see if anyone needed help. It turns out he was a plainclothes police officer. He called for an ambulance and a wrecker. He asked where the people from the other car were. We told him they had taken off walking down the road. He told me to jump into his truck so we could find them.

My company van had packages in it, so I didn't want to leave it there by itself. He didn't hesitate to remind me that he was a police officer who was telling me to lock it up and go with him. Well, okay then. My office was notified, and they said to go.

We didn't see them walking anywhere. Just when we thought they must have caught a ride, we saw them get off a bus. That cop went wild. He jumped the curb, and we went airborne. He yelled for me to pull the emergency brake as we were flying thru the air.

He jumped out of the truck, rolled onto the ground with a shotgun in his hands and shouted, *"Lay down on the ground,"* to those guys. They hit the ground face down fast. All of that happened before his truck could even slide to a stop.

It felt like we were in a Starsky and Hutch television episode. It was so much fun to be a part of catching them. While he had those guys face down on the ground, I remembered my company van. We were at least two or three miles from the wreck. He asked another officer to give me a ride back to my vehicle and thanked me for helping him.

Are you kidding? It was my pleasure! Justice was won that day, and it was a good feeling to watch someone willing to defend that elderly couple.

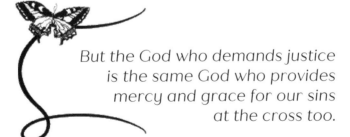

But the God who demands justice is the same God who provides mercy and grace for our sins at the cross too.

You know, that's what God is like. His holy and perfect nature demands justice. That's why Jesus died on the cross to pay for our sins. But the God who demands justice is the same God who provides mercy and grace for our sins at the cross too. Think on that one for a while.

MEN'S RETREAT

"The angel of the LORD encamps all
around those who fear Him,
and delivers them."
PSALM 34:7

THE MEN FROM OUR CHURCH used to go to an annual retreat together. There were dorms that slept about eight guys. Here we are, all of us guy buddies in the same room for the weekend.

Lord, help us! One of them wouldn't go to sleep until he had a glass of water. He laid there calling out his wife's name, like a bleating sheep, asking for water over and over again. We got so tired of hearing him that someone finally got him one. They poured it all over him. We all got a laugh out of that except him. It was fun acting like kids again.

We also had the Big Pig Shoot Out basketball game. There were two teams of three guys playing against each other. Our pastor was an Arkansas Razorback fan, and he would wear his Big Pig hat to retreat. That's why it was called the Big Pig Shoot Out. We also competed with horseshoes and chess tournaments. We played other games, all with a trophy to win.

It was a pretty competitive weekend, but the Big Pig Shoot Out was the biggest deal. Whoever won the shootout took a big trophy home to their church for display until the next retreat. We did this at every men's retreat for many years.

This year, the pastor flew down in a little airplane. His friend was the pilot. The plane was almost there when the engine stopped, which meant a crash landing. As they were coming down, the pilot saw they were headed for a creek and tried to pull the plane up. He hoped to jump the creek without crashing into it. The left wheel hit something and came off, but they made it over the creek and slid to a safe landing.

They were all okay. The pastor said he had to go pee when he got out because the crash scared it right out of him. They got someone to fix the wheel while they were at retreat. We asked them if they were really going to fly back on the same plane. They said yes. It turned out the pilot didn't check the fuel level before they left so it had run out. They made sure it had plenty of fuel for the return flight.

The camp also had a fishing pond so we could fish whenever we wanted. All we had to bring was our fishing gear. They provided the boats. We spent a lot of time out on that pond with our buddies.

Oh! By the way, I won that horseshoe tournament a few times. The secret to winning is to find the oldest guy there and get him to be your partner. Those older guys know how to catch fish and play horseshoes!

Some of us rode our motorcycles to the retreat because it was a beautiful ride in the country. One time it was storming hard when the retreat was over. The ride shouldn't have been too bad with raingear, but traffic from Dallas to Houston was bumper-to-bumper down the interstate that Sunday afternoon.

It was raining so hard you couldn't see the road well, even with a windshield. I pulled over and started riding slowly along the side of the highway hoping to see better.

There was some construction ahead, and the highway made a curve to the right. The shoulder became the highway where it curved so my lane of travel came to an end. Cars were flying past me, and there was no way to merge back in. My back tire was bald so it might not get good traction. The bike might spin and hit a car on the highway.

I didn't know what to do but decided to take the bike into the shallow creek alongside the highway. It might sink, but it made better sense than walking home and leaving the bike on the side of the road for someone to steal. So, I pointed it toward the creek and gave it some gas.

When it hit the water, it also hit a big rock. The rock caused the bike to shoot up out of the creek and onto the feeder. It slid a little but landed upright. There were no cars on the road where it landed either. Mud covered me and the bike from head to toe, but it was raining so hard that it washed it all away. The trip home was a safe ride.

He's a good, good God.
I hope you know that.

There was an angel riding shotgun on my bike that day. There was an angel riding shotgun for my pastor and his friend also. Can you think of a time when there might have been an angel riding shotgun with you?

Think that doesn't happen? Think again. God says that when we make the Lord our dwelling place, He places His angels to watch over us. Check out what it says in Psalm 91. You'll like reading how God takes care of you. He's a good, good God. I hope you know that.

HOMELESS WITH KIDS

"Then the righteous will answer Him,
saying, "Lord, when did we see You hungry
and feed You, or thirsty and give You
drink? ...And the King will answer and say
to them, "Assuredly, I say to you, inasmuch
as you did it to one of the least of these
My brethren, you did it to Me."
MATTHEW 25:37-40

WHEN OUR DAUGHTER was in middle school, we started taking our church youth group into downtown Houston to feed the homeless. We met at the church to have prayer first. Then we made thirty or forty sack lunches with sandwiches, chips and fruit. We loaded a couple of cars with kids and headed downtown.

On the first trip, we were hunting for where the homeless hung out. When I got out of the car to talk to a couple of homeless guys, the kids locked the doors. It's good they were thinking of safety, but they were too scared to unlock the door and let me back in. Did they forget who was driving the car?

When they finally unlocked the car, we had a talk. We had asked God to go before us, and we knew He would. We were in a group and would stick together. Everything was going to be okay.

We walked down under the Main Street Bridge where several people were living. The kids started offering lunches to them. They were excited to see young teens handing out food. The kids got more comfortable talking with them, and we had a great day telling them about Jesus. By the time we were done, the kids decided they loved feeding the homeless, so we kept returning.

There was a time we went downtown in a van to feed them, and I forgot my wallet at home. I didn't realize that until after we had left, and we were out of gas now. My plan was to fuel up while we were out but leaving my wallet at home made that hard. We didn't have cell phones to call for help back then. There were no pay phones either.

One of the homeless guys heard us talking. He went around and collected spare change from all the homeless that were sitting around there. They came over to our van and told us they heard about us being out of gas with no cash, and they took up a collection for us. They gave us a few dollars in change to get gas with. It really touched my heart to think they would give up their last dime to help us. Their kindness came from their heart, and it's how we got back to the church that day.

The teens tried to talk them into giving up their wine bottles whenever they could. That wasn't easy since alcohol is really important to a lot of homeless. Some of the bottles they gave to the kids still had wine in them, so you know the decision had really meant something to that person. We told them Jesus had a better way, and the kids encouraged them to trust God to help them give it up for just one day and then another until they saw that they could give it up for good with God's help.

The kids got so comfortable talking with them that it was tough to keep up with them. They couldn't wait to go downtown to feed and pray with them again. They would jump out of the car and take off running. We needed a fishing pole to reel them in. They were so eager to help these people.

On another day, we were giving out socks. Socks and underwear are often hard for people on the street to get. We found a grocery cart to load all the socks into and got ready to bless as many people as we could. Only one pair each because they sometimes sell their extra pair to buy drugs and alcohol.

As we were walking with the socks, a big guy came over and demanded all of them. We weren't going to fight him over socks, so we gave them to him. The kids were upset about it, but God takes care of you when you're serving Him.

A group of people came over asking for socks after this guy left. We told them we used to have some but that guy over there took them all. They went over to the guy with all the socks and asked for them back. It was ten against one, so he gave them up. They brought the socks back to us and everyone got a new pair. God blessed our efforts without a fight.

Once we took some of the teens downtown late at night so they could see what living on the streets was really like. Some of the parents were having trouble with their kids and wanted them to understand why they didn't want to end up on the streets. We were trying to encourage them to stay in school and learn something to help them with life.

One kid in our youth group had everything a kid could want, and he also had a better-than-you attitude toward people who didn't have as much as he did. His parents wanted him to get a feel for how hard life was for people on the streets, so we came up with this plan to help the kids see.

There was a particular area downtown that had a lot of homeless teens. It was a crowded place, and these kids were wild. We wanted our teens to see the world but never allowed them out of the car here for their safety. The teenagers in this area were selling their bodies for sex in order to get money to pay for drugs. They were doing drugs openly and having sex inside cars along the street. It wasn't unusual to see people carrying guns and fighting.

We pulled up to a place at the end of a road where there was a club full of cars and people in the parking lot. As we were leaving, the kids saw a couple of guys together on the porch. None of them had seen anything like the things going on here before. The kids were all pretty quiet on the way back to the church.

The one with the attitude thanked me for taking him. It changed his life. He became friendlier with the other kids. His parents said he was more appreciative of his family and the things he had.

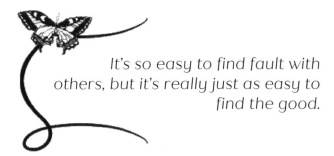

It's so easy to find fault with others, but it's really just as easy to find the good.

We spent a lot of time with the homeless and youth groups over the years. We put them all into God's hands long ago and know He will continue to take care of them. We ran into one of the kids from our youth group years later. She was still going downtown to minister to the homeless and was taking her own children with her now.

It's rewarding to know she kept it going on for the Lord and used experiences from her youth to teach her children about serving God. We took our children with us for this ministry too. It was good for them to see these things. One night our son complained about what he was having for dinner and our daughter reminded him to be thankful for what he had because some people were having to find their dinner on the streets.

These were good life lessons. Jesus challenged us all to reach out to the world. The gospel message sounds much sweeter when it's backed by faith in action. It's so easy to find fault with others, but it's really just as easy to find the good.

We had some great youth who really loved the Lord, and we praise God for the time we shared with them. It was our privilege to watch these kids, and our own, grow in their faith.

NEVER GIVE UP ON PEOPLE

"So then neither he who plants is anything,
Nor he who waters, but God who gives
the increase."
I CORINTHIANS 3:7

WE WORKED with homeless people on the streets of Houston for many years. Some of them were easy to deal with. Others were not. One time when we took our church youth group to minister downtown, we met two guys who lived in the penthouse of a high-rise apartment building.

Well, that's what they called it. It was really just a rusty staircase on the outside of an old rundown building. It was home to them, and they seemed to love it there. You know, sometimes we don't really need as much as we think we do to be happy. Our youth group began to understand this as we shared scriptures and prayed for the people we met.

This was a time of ministry to the homeless, but it was also a time of learning and growing in faith for our youth. It was a time of learning and growing for me as well.

As God gave us opportunities, we were there. What a blessing to be able to help meet their needs. The two guys who lived in the stairwell were there so often we got to know them pretty good. After a while, my wife agreed we could take them home for showers.

So, they began coming home with us. We bought clothes for them, fed them and got their hair cut. They began to come quite often. Eventually, we even asked them to watch our house for us while we went on vacation. They had a real bed to sleep in for a couple of weeks. We left some food in the refrigerator for them and hit the road.

They took good care of the house for us. We thanked them and gave them some money for taking care of the house. Later on, they came to live with us for a few months.

Sometimes we don't really need as much as we think we do to be happy.

You never know where your path will lead. We witnessed to these guys for several years. It seemed like we weren't reaching them with the gospel. Eventually, they both moved away. One went one way, and one went another. They kept in touch with us for a long time after they moved.

One of them had health issues and was in a hospital the last time we spoke with him. He wasn't doing well, and we don't know what happened to him. We're thankful for the time we were able to spend sharing the love of Christ with him though.

The other one got married. He still came to visit when he was in town. His mother passed away and left him a lot of money. He started blowing it everywhere. He bought a house, a boat, a van and started making beer in his home. He started doing drugs again, and he lost everything. The bank foreclosed on the house, and he sold the boat. He and his wife took off living in their van.

He was unhappy and called collect all the time to talk about his troubles. Collect calls weren't bad as long as we could afford them. When a back injury kept me from working, the calls had to stop. There was no money to keep paying for his calls. He kept calling for a while, but we refused them, so he stopped. A seed was planted in his heart though.

A few years later, his wife called to let me know he had died. She had come back to Houston to bury him and wanted to talk with me while she was in town. She said my family was the only one that would help them when they were really down, and it meant a lot to them. She told me they didn't know what to do when we stopped taking their calls because no one else cared. She said that's when they knew their lives were really bad and decided it was time to serve the Lord.

They got involved with a church where they were living and straightened their lives up. Her husband was teaching Bible studies for the church when he died. An aneurysm to the brain killed him. She said he often told people about how our family helped them when they were on the streets.

They were helping the homeless now. She said they wanted to call and tell us how they were doing but had not done it. She didn't want to go back home without thanking us for not giving up on them. That's what it felt like we were doing when we refused their calls. She said not to feel that way because God used it to help them realize they needed Him.

Folks, all we do is water and plant. We're His hands and feet in ministry. We're His face to the world around us, but it's God who saves and changes people. He's the caretaker. He draws the hearts. We cannot. Praise God that He loves us as we are, and I'm so thankful that He doesn't give up on us.

THE KIDS ON OUR BLOCK

"The fear of man brings a snare, but
whoever trusts in the LORD shall be safe."
PROVERBS 29:25

WE LIVED ON A CUL-DE-SAC while our kids were growing up and our house was always full of kids. Some of these kids said we were like their second parents, and we loved them like they were our own kids. One of our neighbors had four kids who hung out at our house a lot. Their mom ran off with another guy and left them with their stepdad while they lived there. He worked nights so the kids were on their own after dark a lot. We tried to be there for them as best we could while they were alone.

One night the oldest daughter called us to help with a gang of kids who wouldn't leave their house. Being woke up in the middle of the night didn't always feel great, but we wanted people to know they could call us any time they needed help, especially if they were kids.

My first reaction was to call the cops. They were already at their house when I got there. Kids were scattering everywhere, jumping fences and running into the woods to get away. The police had some guys leaning up against cars.

Walking up to the front door, a kid handed me a beer as he ran out. An officer walked over and asked if the beer belonged to me. It didn't, but we talked about what was going on with the kids.

My daughter's friend introduced me as the neighbor she had called to help get the guys to leave. The cops still had the guys leaning against their car. One of the guys kept saying this was all my fault. What made him think that? I told him they had done it to themselves, and he responded with a threat.

That made me mad so I asked the officer if he could let me handle that guy. For some reason, he didn't agree with that idea. The kid kept threatening me. I told him not to let the cops stop him and was so irritated with him that there probably would have been a fight if the cops had not been there to stop it. The police suggested it might be best for me to go home.

The cop stopped by to talk with me before leaving. He said the guy who threatened me was bad news. He was the primary suspect for a recent drive-by shooting in our area. The cop felt he might come back for me and suggested we should leave for the night. I told him no one was going to chase me out of my own home.

He gave me his card and said to call if he showed up. He even joked that he would come pick up the body if he happened to get shot. He advised me to carry a gun in my truck for a while in case he came around looking for trouble. My family went to stay with my in-laws that night.

It seemed like getting our kids out was the smart thing to do. I stayed home with my gun waiting for him to show back up. That probably wasn't so smart, but he never came back. They finally did arrest that young man for killing someone though.

Sometimes it's not easy to trust God, even as a Christian, especially when your family is in danger. As parents, you're supposed to teach your children. I may have learned more from being a parent than my kids ever learned from having me as their dad. My home life certainly had not prepared me for parenting. God had to teach me a lot all along the way. This was definitely one of those times. I'm glad my kids and their friends felt they could come to me for help, but my temper and pride kept me from making a good decision. My emotions should not have been allowed to control me like they did that night. It could have put my family in real danger, and it certainly wasn't a good Christian witness.

God could have been trusted to take care of things rather than trying to handle everything myself. I knew that but, in the moment, it wasn't what I was thinking about. Sometimes we just act like the humans we are. When you make a mistake, you have to own it. So, I made sure these kids knew my decisions that night weren't the best ones, and that I should have trusted God to take handle it. You'll never go wrong when you choose to place your life in His hands.

A MOST EMBARRASSING MOMENT

"As obedient children do not conform to
the evil desires you had when you lived in
ignorance. But just as he who called you is
holy, so be holy in all you do."
1 PETER 1:14-15 (NIV)

DO YOU REMEMBER your most embarrassing moment in life? Everyone has at least one that sticks out more than any other. If your friends were asked for a story about you, we would probably find your moment too. Well, here's mine.

My best friend was crazy like me, so we had fun everywhere we went. We had known each other for many years. We were living miles apart at the time, so our families took turns taking trips to see each other. We did lots of stuff together and kept our kids entertained. Our wives said we weren't good examples, but the kids said we were fun. Our wives still loved us for some reason, even though we drove them crazy.

We were goofing around at a grocery store one day when he took a piece of gum from his mouth and wadded it into my arm hair. My arm would have to be shaved to get it off. That was going to require payback, and this was a great chance to get it.

I was bent way over with my head in the back of the cooler looking for ice cream, and my friend was standing behind me. At least, it seemed like he was standing there. Yeah, this was going to be good.

There was a huge...um...gasser?...in my gut just waiting for the best moment to get him back. I hiked my leg up to let loose on him and then heard my friend laughing from the other end of the aisle. So, who was behind me? The lady standing there looked horrified. She said "OH...MY...GOD!"

My head went back into the freezer not wanting to come out. Ever! She walked away, and I ran over to hit my friend. She saw me coming down another aisle later and went the other way. Who could blame her? It was really embarrassing for both of us.

Manners weren't talked about around me growing up. My manners were learned in a bar. There weren't many well-mannered people there to learn from. Some people wondered if I would ever learn how to act. My lack of manners drove my father-in-law nuts. He was raised with better manners than me.

The most important things about how to conduct myself were learned by studying God's Word. There's true transforming power within those pages. Oh, to be like Jesus! He's perfect, and the greatest teacher you'll ever find.

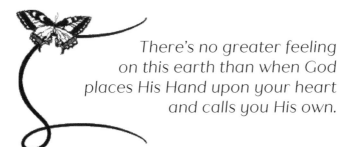

There's no greater feeling on this earth than when God places His Hand upon your heart and calls you His own.

Like I said before, you'll never hear me claim to be perfect. There are too many faults and failures in my life. My desire is to be more like Jesus every day. That's what I hope people will remember most about me.

If that's your desire, it starts with a simple prayer. The one where you ask Jesus to forgive your failures. When you do, He'll make your heart His home. You'll feel at home with that too. There's no greater feeling on this earth than when God places His Hand upon your heart and calls you His own.

FASTEN YOUR SEATBELT

"...let us lay aside every weight, and the sin which so easily ensnares us, and let us run with endurance the race that is set before us, looking unto Jesus, the author and finisher of our faith..."
HEBREWS 12:1

SOME PASTORS TOLD ME that one of the ways you know God is calling you to preach is that you want to finish the sermon for the preacher because you have a burning feeling there's so much more to be said. We were blessed to sit under some of the best men of God that ever lived as our pastors. They inspired me with a love for the Word of God, and I wanted to preach the gospel, too.

It became my prayer to ask God to use me this way, if it was His will. When God wanted me to do something, He often confirmed it to me either by showing my wife as well or giving me stepping stones to get it done. That's what happened when God used us to start a church.

One of my friends in the air freight business used to joke with me about my faith as a Christian. He always tried to tell me the Bible said things it didn't so we would have a friendly discussion about it. He never gave in, but we could laugh about it.

One day, the engine on our car blew up, and it needed a new motor. We hadn't told anyone about our car, but this friend came up to me at work with an envelope. He said God told him to give it to me as a gift and that I shouldn't refuse. There was a check inside for exactly the amount needed to buy the engine for our car. That was amazing. He always said he wasn't a Christian, and yet God chose to use him to minister to my family.

We talked a lot about how much God loved him and died on a cross for him so he could go to heaven. He would laugh because he didn't believe it. I still reminded him every chance I could that He would have done that for him, even if he was the only person on the planet.

We laughed and joked sometimes that we couldn't understand why because he certainly didn't deserve it. The truth is that none of us deserve what God did for us at the cross.

Eventually, we both changed jobs and lost touch for a while. Several years later, we ran into each other again at a grocery store. We talked about how we had missed seeing each other. He asked what we were doing now so I told him we were praying about starting a church.

My minister's license had been received a few years back, and we were serving in ministry but not as senior pastor. He said to start the church and he would come. That meant a lot coming from this guy. My wife and I continued to pray for God's will about that.

One day while out shopping for a suit at a resale shop, a man and his wife came into the store. They stood out because they were all dressed up. She went to the ladies' section, and he walked to the men's area near me. He asked if I was a minister, and I replied yes. He said he felt like God wanted him to pray for me and asked if it would be okay.

Well, anytime someone wants to pray for me, it's alright! When he finished praying, he said God wanted him to tell me something. He said, *"God said to fasten your seatbelt because you're fixing to go for a ride in your ministry."*

That sounded pretty cool, but I didn't really think too much about it. People say a lot of things sometimes. We went back to shopping and then they were gone.

Later, while working in the men's section of a department store, a gentleman came up to me and asked if we had hats. He told me his hair was falling out from chemo treatments. He needed a hat to keep his head warm during the cold months. He looked around and found one he liked.

When he came to pay, we talked about some medical tests being scheduled for me. He asked if he and his wife could pray for me. Well, of course, he could! We prayed and then he said God wanted him to tell me something. It was, *"Fasten your seatbelt because you're fixing to go for a ride in your ministry."*

It made me a little dizzy. They helped me to a chair where we talked about the guy saying the exact thing just a few months ago. That was an exciting day.

A short time later, we formed the Journey of Grace Fellowship Church. It wasn't too long after we started it when a guy made an offer to let us have one of his buildings to rent. He wasn't a Christian, but he was excited about having a church there. He added rooms for children's church, a restroom and a front porch.

Then he said he was planning a surprise for our first day in the new building. We didn't have chairs to sit on the day before our meeting, and we didn't know what to do. We also had a funeral to attend out of town that day, so we were pressed for time.

After the funeral, we went to the pastor's house to visit with the family but were in a hurry to leave. The pastor asked why we needed to leave so soon, so we told him about the chairs. He asked what color and how many chairs we needed. Well, we needed thirty beige chairs. To our surprise, he said, *"If you had thirty beige chairs, would you stay a little longer?"*

We joked that would sure make it easier to stay. He took me to his church where he had thirty beige chairs with padding that they were trying to get rid of. He said we could have them for free. Wow! When we got back to the church, I cried while unloading those chairs. They were perfect, just like the God who provided them for us.

When we get to our home in heaven one day, there will be some beautiful bells ringing a celebration song for us all!

The next morning, I went to the new church building a little early for prayer and coffee before everyone showed up. There was a hangman's noose on the porch. It might have been a joke, but it didn't seem funny to me. When I tried to pull it down, a bell rang. Well, the owner had said he would have a surprise for us on Sunday. How cool!

It wasn't a noose after all. He had put a bell on the porch for us to ring on Sunday mornings. It wasn't little either. It was a big, loud iron bell. He may have been sorry about that later because he was the only person living around there. I gladly woke him up every Sunday morning with the church bell God had provided. We loved the sound of that bell!

Oh, and the guy who worked with me in air freight? Yes, he came to that church. He gave his life to the Lord there and became one of our first members. What a blessing this church was!

We were honored to pastor this church for five years. We learned so much about the life of a pastor and his wife from our experiences there. The most exciting of these experiences was to witness someone accepting Jesus as their Lord. We joined some in marriage and, hopefully, played a part in saving others. Babies were dedicated. Believers were baptized. God's Word was taught. Friendships were made.

We learned the importance of supporting your pastor and his wife in prayer faithfully. Their lives go through things that you will never be able to hear about as their congregation, which is the way it should be because they're dealing with the private things that are happening in your lives. They need you as much as you need them. Together, we form the body of Christ.

The five years with our church were some of the most rewarding years of our life. We met some beautiful souls there. When we get to our home in heaven one day, there will be some beautiful bells ringing a celebration song for us all! What a beautiful day that will be.

WHAT I BELIEVE

*"Jesus answered and said to him, "If
anyone loves Me, he will keep My word;
and My Father will love him, and We will
come to him and make Our
home with him."*
JOHN 14:23

PEOPLE BELIEVE in many things. You can be Christian, Baptist, Methodist, Catholic, Assembly of God, Pentecostal, Mormon, Agnostic or Atheist. You can be Buddhist, Hindu, Muslim, Wiccan, Satanic or many other religions. Someone once said religion is merely man's search for God. Religion is not what we need. What we need is a relationship with God thru Jesus, His Only Son.

Some people don't believe the Bible is the infallible Word of God. For many years, people have tried to destroy the Bible. That will not happen because it is the Word of God. The Bible is where your relationship with Jesus begins.

People often turn from one religion to another. You will not see many turning from Christ once they've found a true relationship with Him. I believe He is the answer to man's search for God. The Bible says you will find Him when you search for Him with all of your heart.

Some of you may not agree with me but let me tell you why I believe what I believe. See, I hated pretty much everyone on earth except my sister, but she never did anything to make me mad at her. Most people didn't like me because there wasn't much to like about me.

Drinking and drugs made me a hateful, bitter person. Vodka and weed were my friends in elementary school. Heavy drugs joined them shortly after. I popped pills without even asking what they were because I didn't care.

You see, living wasn't for me. I tried to kill myself more than once. Jumping off a baseball backstop headfirst didn't break my neck. It just gave me a bad headache. Jumping in front of a car only scratched me.

A box of asthma pills only made me watch the ceiling breathe all night. I tried everything looking for purpose and truth in life. I got high and took off hitchhiking across the United States. I joined the big circus and traveled on their train. I even joined the Army and that didn't help. Looking for a gun to blow my brains out with didn't work either. I didn't know what else to do.

I hope this story hasn't bored you, but you should know the person who is writing this book. There's nothing fake about me. What you see is what you get. I'm just your basic booger-head! I didn't go to school much so didn't get much of an education.

It's hard to believe I'm even writing this book. It's having to be rewritten due to my bad spelling, bad grammar and run-on sentences. But my kids have asked me for many years to share my testimony in a book for others to read. I decided to do it for several reasons. It's being shared so my kids will remember their dad's life and my grandkids will know their grandpa a little better.

Also, so it might be used by God to reach someone's heart so they will find Jesus as their Lord and Savior, because I love Jesus and want to tell others what He's done for me. And, because I believe this is what God wants me to do.

My life hasn't been the same since the day Jesus came into it. He has blessed me beyond anything ever thought possible. I've been married to the most wonderful woman in the world for over forty years now.

We have two precious kids, a daughter and a son, who are now adults. Their husband and wife are my kids too. I love them both like they are my own. We have six grandkids. One is with Jesus today. The rest are driving me crazy. Just kidding! They are all loved with all of my heart. My family means the world to me.

In 2016, my aortic valve had to be replaced and my kidneys failed after surgery. They had me unconscious on life support for ten days and didn't know if I would live. So, they tell me this story almost didn't get a chance to be written.

But as long as there is breath in this body, I will be preaching where I can. I really believe God spared me so this story could be shared with you. I hope it blesses you as much as it has blessed me to write it and pray it speaks to people about Jesus long after I'm gone.

Remember, it's not about religion. It's about relationship. Don't follow the church. Follow Christ. It doesn't matter where you go to church. It matters if you ARE the church. The Bible is true, and it is absolute. It is the infallible Word of God, and it says God loves you. It says He created you and intends good things for you.

One of those good things includes the perfect home in heaven He has prepared for you. We tend to put a lot of time into accomplishing something with our lives here on earth, but this world is not our home. We will all leave it behind one day.

Shortly after we were married, I woke my wife up in the middle of the night. She says I asked her to say "yes." She asked what for, and I told her to just say "yes."

We did this several times. Tired, she gave in and agreed. I turned over and went back to sleep, but now she was awake and wondering what she had agreed to. So, now she woke me up and asked. She says I told her, *"Oh, you just agreed we're going to heaven together."* I didn't remember it the next morning, but it was in my dreams, so it must have been important for me to know a home in heaven was in her future.

God's desire is for you to share a forever home with Him in eternity. It's important to Him, but He leaves the decision to you. It's a decision only you can make. No one can decide who the Lord of your heart is but you. Jesus is knocking at the door of the home in your heart. So, what do you say? Will you invite Him in?

So many reasons to smile!

BUTTERFLIES

ERNIE'S SON AND GRANDCHILDREN provided these original works of art in honor of his request to remember his new life whenever we see butterflies in our lives. It makes us smile to find one of these beautiful creatures near us now, and we see them often. We hope you'll begin to notice them around you, too, as a reminder that the love of Jesus surrounds you with the hope of new life and new beginnings as you journey home.

IN MEMORY

ERNIE DEPARTED THIS LIFE for his home in heaven on November 11, 2018. Some have shared a few "stories" of their own with you here in remembrance of how their lives were touched by his. To this, we are certain Ernie would say, "To God be the glory; great things He has done."

"My dad has finally heard the words, "Well done, thy good and faithful servant." Heaven gained one special angel. I know he will be watching over us and sending nuggets of comfort from time to time. I will miss him forever and will always be a daddy's girl! Mount up on wings and soar!" – Joy

"Dad, I love you with everything I have, and I couldn't have had a better example of a father. I thank God every day for that. I'm going to miss you so much that it hurts my soul, but I have comfort that I know you aren't suffering anymore. Heaven got a great one! I love you forever." – Josh

"For the past 19 years, I have been privileged to be a part of this man's life. He accepted me as a son and loved me as one of his own children. He was gracious enough to give away his only daughter's hand in marriage to me. He was truly one of the sweetest, most selfless men I have ever met and was a great example of how to be a leader in Christ, to be a great husband, father, grandfather and friend. We will miss you more than words can describe." - Brent

"I met Ernie in Little Rock at a pizza parlor in the 70's where we worked. I have given his testimony of the power of the Word of God healing his mind. His mind had been destroyed by drugs when he came to the Lord. But he was saved by the grace of God

and able to read the Bible. By reading it constantly, his mind was restored. I'll never forget this man of God."

"He was the most caring, thoughtful, compassionate, Jesus loving, man of God. He lit up any room with his smile, his love for God and people, and especially with his sense of humor. I can't imagine my life without his presence and influence. This man has been such a blessing in my life, I don't even know where to begin. Growing up he was like a second dad. He loved me unconditionally, prayed for me, led me spiritually as my pastor, baptized me and so much more. The thing is, he has done the same for so many others. God has definitely said, 'Well done, my good and faithful servant.' We love you, Ernie!"

"When my daughter was in the hospital, Ernie gave my daughter a very special stuffed animal. It meant the world to me that he came and prayed over my daughter. He always had a sense of humor and a big smile and hug for us. We were so thankful to be included in his life.

"Ernie is one of the greatest men I've ever known. It was an honor to know him here on earth. I can truly say my life and my family were irrevocably changed when Ernie and his amazing family came into our lives. A personality larger than life – that was Ernie. He's probably already made Jesus a whole menagerie of balloon animals and I wouldn't put it past him to try and pull a quarter out of Saint Peter's ear. I will miss his smile and zest for life. You will NEVER be forgotten.

"There are so many great things I can say about Ernie. He is by far the best friend a girl could ask for and the best part is that he didn't have to be. I love you Ernie. Always and forever in our hearts."

"I'm honored to have been loved by him and to have had the privilege of loving him in return. Sometimes it only takes one person to change your life. One to be there for you, to push you, to believe in you. It only takes one. You were that person to so many people and I think you were too humble to even know it. All you wanted was to allow God to work through you and He did. You are loved beyond measure. You didn't know but I gave up when I lost my mom and you're what kept me here. You were a blessing to so many and when I think of God's love in action, I always think of you."

"He taught me to not fear or be sad but instead rejoice for those who pass on. I am forever grateful."

"Ernie helped me to be a better person. He told me all of the trials in his life when he was younger and helped me get out of the same lifestyle."

"Late night games, milkshakes, magic tricks, great storyteller, gripping testimony, never met a stranger, friends and fun with love of family and Jesus. He was a joy here and in joy now. He touched my life."

"Many people wonder what their legacy will reflect. Some people care and some don't. Ernie only cared about what his Savior thought. Don't get me wrong, he loved everyone. His heart's desire is for everyone to know Jesus and God's peace, love, joy and happiness. He mentioned he would not change a thing about his life before meeting the love of his life, Julie. Ernie shared his childhood days with all that would listen in hopes of leading souls to Christ. He was a straight-shooter, no-sugar-coating type of man when it came to heaven or hell. Ernie performed our wedding 18 years ago. The one thing I remember him telling us was to put God first. Only fitting our daughter's baby dedication would be performed by Ernie. I admired Ernie for being the type of man that practiced what he preached. Ernie's legacy will forever live on in his family and for all who are blessed by Ernie's friendship."

"Heaven received a beautiful angel today. I'm gonna miss your smile and corny balloon animals. You always knew how to cheer up a room and make everyone laugh. I've looked up to your positivity and selflessness. Even though cancer won, I admired you for staying strong. Love you forever and always!"

"My memory of Ernie is taking a person off the street and trying to change his life by mentoring him and bringing him into his home. He surely did that more than once. I know he is so happy now with no pain and no sickness and is receiving the many crowns God has for him in heaven."

"In 2001, it was time to make God a part of my life so me and my wife started searching for a church. I prayed and called several churches. When Ernie answered the phone, there was something in that man's voice that drew me, and he impacted my life. I will forever love, miss and call him my best friend."

"He was special. I will cherish the memories we made. You were funny, always smiling and laughing. You always knew how to cheer someone up, saw the brightness in every day. You loved the Lord more than just about anyone I know. I had the pleasure of you baptizing me at your church. I love you and will miss you more than you could imagine. Thank you for being there and loving me unconditionally."

"Ernie prayed for people, even when he didn't know them. He was an inspiration, not afraid to tell people about Jesus, and he did that a lot. We talked about God and I learned so much. He was a great friend. He liked working in the city park because he met people and was able to pray with them. He fed the hungry. He never got tired of people. He did balloon animals, magic tricks and *made kids and adults laugh. He had the greatest stories and a great testimony. I was broken and he lifted me up. I wasn't living right and then was saved. He married my husband and I ten years ago. I believed in him and he believed in me like a friend should. See you in heaven my friend."*

"Ernie was crazy. Even when he didn't agree, he never judged. He listened. He didn't always understand my decisions, but he was always supportive and loved me anyway.

"My best friend and I are Spanish teachers. No one in our family speaks Spanish, so in order to keep up with our Spanish skills, we decided to go to Mexico and take lessons. We didn't plan on bad weather on the trip home. We were stranded at the Houston airport. There were no flights and every hotel was sold out. I told my friend I was going to call Ernie. I did and it went something like this.... Hi Ernie, what are you doing? He said I'm at work. I said my friend and I are stranded at the airport and were wondering if we could sleep on your couch. He said hold on. He got back on the phone and said you're in Houston, right? I said yes, and he said hold on. He returned to the phone and I said what's going on? He said I just quit my job, and I'm coming to get you. And he did."

"Ernie had the best stories to tell. When I lost everything and had to walk to work in winter, he bought me a jacket, gloves and hat. He said he would drive me and, if he couldn't, at least I wouldn't be cold."

"My husband and I worked with Ernie at the school when he was also pastor at Journey of Grace. We were engaged and wanted to ask him to marry us. Neither of us were attending church and decided to attend his before we asked him to marry us. We knew God was pulling us in, and we became a part of JOG. Ernie and his wife taught me who Jesus is and why I needed him. He and his

family "walk the walk" of true followers of Jesus and modeled unconditional love for us all. We loved his stories. He was so full of joy you couldn't help but be happy around him. One night Ernie came over and led me to Christ. Ernie helped my husband and me through some tough times. Ernie's genuine kindness, wisdom, love for people and passion for the gospel will be an inspiration for me forever. "I press on toward the goal to win the prize for which God has called me heaven ward in Jesus Christ." Philippians 3:14

"Ernie was amazing and inspiring. The things he would frequently say and do that showed his passion and compassion for young people and for the homeless were ubiquitous. I don't think there was a visit I ever had with him where he did not bring up something to do with his love for connecting people with Jesus and also for meeting their physical and emotional needs. That stands as a towering example and inspiration for me that I don't believe will ever fade."

"Ernie was such a bright light in this world, and he was such a blessing. A couple years ago, when the kids were in baseball, he was at one of the games. I will never forget that encounter. I had never spent time around him, but he spoke to me like I was a dear family friend. Like me & him had somehow been buddies in a past life. He was just like that I've come to learn. That day he made me laugh, and he told me to find and focus on my joy. He said, "find your joy...I found mine." And then he looked at his daughter and winked. He loved his kids and his wife, grandkids, me, strangers.... Life! He showed God's love and kindness every time I saw him. I am blessed and inspired to witness that."

"Ernie helped so, so many people. His actions, his words, his love were all the true representation of Jesus Christ. What a beautiful person. I am so happy to have met him years ago and loved him dearly."

"How do I describe it? Awe inspiring? Infectious or overwhelming perhaps? I had never been around someone who was annoyingly, yet oddly happy. It's not a bad annoying by any means. No, it's one of those I'm jealous because my life sucks and how dare you be so happy annoying. I remember this over joyous fella introducing himself to me. Walked up, shook my hand and gave me a hug. I open with small talk and somehow, we made it to my beliefs.

I learned Ernie never met a stranger. I've never seen that in my life, so it freaked me out a bit. My girlfriend let me know her family were Christians. They were genuine folks. They wouldn't judge me, and I was to be prepared for hugs. So far so good. Ernie and I are talking motorcycles and Jesus. I'm pretty sure there's a show out there about that; if not, there should be. He goes into telling me about his past and how he was saved. I didn't get it at the time.

I figured he met a hot chick and turned his life around. Funny how that happens. Fast forward a few years. I'm married to my girlfriend, her family, and Ernie Gober. He's unapologetically a part of my life. I'd sit there dumbfounded asking, uh, is life really a box of chocolates all the time for Ernie? He's always glowing and carefree.

I'd ask, "Hey man, seriously, what is it that you're smoking?" He'd laugh and start talking about Jesus. Really, again? "How about you and me go down a few brewskies then you can let me in on it?" Again, with Jesus talk. Ok, I've seen this show enough to know it was going to end with Jesus talk.

One thing was certain, Ernie had the same sheen as always. Years roll by and life is life. It's challenging roller coaster moments made for Hallmark. I'm struggling with it. I have a young family, a young wife, I'm young. Mistakes are made. I made life chaos an art form. Throughout the ride, we had a cheerleader: Ernie - magic tricks and all. "Ernie's insane," I'd say. No way he can keep up with everyone's mess and do life.

He was always, and I mean always there for everyone. In 2007, I figured out what Ernie's secret was. I got saved. It really was Jesus. It's said those with larger debt are more grateful for that debt being repaid than those with less debt. Grace is truly love, and salvation is priceless.

I will forever be grateful God put Ernie in my life. Ernie's light shown bright through darkness, good times, challenges and heartache. There's always little nuggets and takeaways that some call wisdom or as I call it, life fails made whole. Ernie's nugget to me was this: Never give up on family, friends, nor enemies that God has put in your life. Be patient, God just may use you to be that conduit of blessing to reach the unreachable!"

Made in the USA
Lexington, KY
01 November 2019